THE ROOTS OF JAPANESE ARCHITECTURE

The Roots of

with text and commentaries

A WEATHERMARK EDITION

JAPANESE ARCHITECTURE

a photographic quest by YUKIO FUTAGAWA

by TEIJI ITOH and a foreword by ISAMU NOGUCHI

HARPER & ROW, PUBLISHERS : NEW YORK, EVANSTON, AND LONDON

*This book was originally published in Japanese in 1962 by Bijutsu Shuppan-sha
under the title* Nihon Kenchiku no Ne. *The present text, entirely rewritten by
the author for this English edition, has been translated by Paul Konya and adapted
for Western readers by the editorial staff of John Weatherhill, Inc., Tokyo.*

FIRST EDITION

Library of Congress catalog card number: 63-16240

TABLE OF CONTENTS

FOREWORD
by Isamu Noguchi

The audacity of this book is not its novelty so much as the surprising degree to which it succeeds: its panoramic view has a shape and method which somehow goes beyond popularization to catch, however obliquely, the spirit underlying ancient Japanese concepts of architecture and space.

Its method is a notable example of the developing technique of photographic language in Japan. As in Japanese painting, here too a detail is often more revealing than a broader canvas. Mr. Futagawa uses all the devices of photography, in an ever-widening variety, with viewpoints never dreamed of in more conventional concepts of space, nor heretofore a part of the vocabulary of its appreciation. Indeed, in their composition such photographs suggest an addition to aesthetic experience and, like the "museum without walls," create a new ghost reality that some may even find more significant than the physical architecture they record.

Such photographs accompanied by an excellent text make a book that is instructive in altogether new and odd ways. The presentation is indirect and impressionistic, and yet, one wonders, by what other means could the authors have approached their elusive quest? It is a very Oriental approach, and to overcome the momentary sense of unfamiliarity that it gives is to appreciate how right it is for the present purpose, how well both photographer and essayist have shown that the strength of a tradition lies in its adaptability to continuous change.

The book beautifully demonstrates that the true roots of Japanese architecture lie in the Japanese relationship to nature. I venture to say that the understanding of wood is more important even than the resultant skill in its structural uses, however much it may please us to recognize the similarities between Japanese methods of wood construction and our own steel engineering. And stone is likewise stone.

Perhaps it is the extremely three-dimensional quality of this study that focuses attention upon the sculptural aspect of this Japanese relationship to nature. If one is to call sculpture the aesthetic of form and space, then leaving aside the utilitarian functions of habitation and horticulture, Japanese architecture is indeed sculpture and can be appreciated as such.

What is the significance of those magnificent temple roofs that rise out of the landscape? The author refers to them as sculptures. Their enclosure is like a sanc-

7

tuary, a dominant object in negative space. The Grand Shrines of Ise are like boats on a beach. The fact of enclosure, not the bare space enclosed, is significant. In these sacred structures the function of the roof may be said to be hierarchic and linked to the land as a whole more than to its own immediate space.

But in the gardens associated with Zen and tea ceremony the enclosure has only to do with privacy, for individual communion and for that special kind of solitude which the Japanese have named *wabi*. Within the limits of such an enclosure, an ideal landscape—what the author has termed a miniature universe—is composed of elements dependent upon and enhanced by each other in asymmetrical counterpoint. The building itself can no longer exist as object except as it participates with the garden—as space. The garden lives with and through the building.

I suggest that the hollow, or negative, space of the building's interior is complemented by the positive forms of the garden. Conversely, a too-dominant exterior of a building precludes strong garden forms, thus inviting formality (*shin*) in the adjoining garden. The temple building of Ryoan-ji as seen from the air in Plate 56 is masculine in character; hence the garden is, appropriately, empty space, which has been enhanced by a formal composition of stones to create an even greater emptiness. On the other hand, where the side or private part of a building is feminine, its garden should be in the more informal (*so*) style, like that seen in the rock garden of Daisen-in (Plate 95).

By these remarks it will be seen that I am taking a somewhat different approach from Mr. Itoh's when he says that the Japanese garden seeks anonymity, that it should be passive and unobtrusive. The passive quality has rather, I think, to do with the individual parts that form the building-garden relationship, where nothing should be so self-assertive as to distract from the whole, so that this whole itself can be said to be a full and meaningful emptiness, to be a complete three-dimensional statement.

It is true that we come to each experience with our own limitations and see only that for which we are prepared. But the reflection we see is not just ourselves. Anonymity is hardly the word, and I hesitate to say "abstract": it is the passage of a man. When we visit Saiho-ji, it is Muso Kokushi, or whoever the builder was, that we see pass by. Think of all the great builders and shapers of Japan's architectural space: it is they who are speaking to us over the centuries, both when we physically walk their gardens and rooms and when we revisit them in the pages of this remarkable book.

INTRODUCTION

"The water of a river flows constantly, and today's water is no longer that of yesterday. Even the bubbles that float in a pool appear and disappear; they do not remain for long." These words by Kamo Chomei, from his 12th-century book of random reflections called the *Hojoki*, may well be applied to architecture. Certainly architectural styles change as relentlessly as the river flows, and that entity known as traditional Japanese architecture is today but a remnant of the past, an antique ruin which modern architects may admire but would hardly seek to imitate. The metaphor is also apt in that Japan's traditional builders never regarded their architecture as a perfect, finished thing but rather as something still in transition, still capable of constantly changing. And yet, as Kamo continues, "the river which flows in this way always swirls where it is supposed to swirl, does it not?" Yes, architectural styles change, but in any valid architecture there always remains an underlying system that gives the architecture its validity, a swirling where it is meant to swirl. A tree may grow in various directions, now this way, now that, but so long as it is firmly rooted it remains triumphantly a tree.

In the pages that follow, then, we intend to give, not a history of Japanese architecture (that has already been written many times and in as many ways), but a sincere record, in photographs speaking largely for themselves and in a brief accompanying essay, of a search for the roots of Japanese architecture, for the system that gave it its validity. If, as we hope to demonstrate, that system was one of the world's great architectural achievements, then a knowledge of its workings cannot but have profound significance for us today as we all—architects, builders, dwellers—seek to create the system that will give contemporary architecture *its* validity.

The Japanese system has both a technical and a philosophical aspect. We shall be concerned here, however, not so much with the specific techniques of Japanese architecture as with the broader, and basically more important, philosophical concepts that have inspired those techniques. From a technical point of view, then, it is probably sufficient to understand that Japanese architecture was first and foremost an architecture of the pillar, the post. All its other remarkable and unique facets stem directly from this one structural fact.

The so-called Middle Ages of Japanese history, beginning in the 12th and ending in the 17th century, was a time of war and devastation, of political chaos and changing social conditions. Like the Italian Renaissance, it was also the time of great artistic advances. Faced with physical dangers on every hand, the people sought spiritual stability in the world of art. And only great and true art could provide

the consolation needed: neither shallow fads nor counterfeit methods could prevail against uncertainty and fear. Hence we find that the great system of Japanese architecture which has come down to us today was gradually developed in this era of war and turbulence.

At the beginning of the Middle Ages there was no longer a perfected style that dominated the architectural scene as there had been in the earlier centuries of stable government and strong religious influences, first of native Shintoism and then of Buddhism from the Asian mainland. During the Middle Ages both physical environment and social conditions changed almost as quickly as they do today. As a result, amid many endeavors and frustrations, the people's demands upon space were likewise constantly in transition. Building materials changed, shapes remained in constant flux to meet changing conditions, and there was no ultimate authority, either political or aesthetic, upon which to rely.

In the face of such conditions some builders simply gave up and tried to run away from reality, creating short-lived novelties. Fortunately, however, there were others who persevered—and made an important discovery. The realization gradually came that the pursuit of architectural shape was useless, that the prime requisite was for a system, a basic structural formula, which could be adapted to any kind of change rather than trying to fix constantly changing functions into the rigid framework of a set shape. The principle of the pillar, already existing in the earlier Japanese architecture, supplied this system. Perfecting it, and also developing the allied system of the *tatami* mat (discussed in Section 6), the Japanese builders of the Middle Ages were finally able to rise above the social chaos that surrounded them and to establish an architectural order that was to remain valid for generations to come, that in fact is in use, though diminishingly so, today.

Turning to the philosophy of Japanese architecture, we are immediately brought face to face with the metaphysical concept of *mu*, the philosophy of "nothingness" or non-relativity, of the identity of opposites. Originally a philosophic-religious concept from China, one that found full flowering in Zen Buddhism and its view that good and evil are but two aspects of the same quality, this philosophy came in time to permeate all Japanese thinking, including Japanese aesthetics. As difficult for the modern, Western-oriented Japanese to understand as for the Westerner himself, it nevertheless was an important part of the cultural air breathed by all Japanese of the time. Among other things, it had a far-reaching effect upon Japanese architecture. Hence its understanding is important for our quest, not because

it was necessarily a better architectural philosophy than those of other times and cultures, but simply because it *was* an integrated philosophy, without which no architecture, ancient or modern, can long be viable.

To speak of "beautifying" a city or to describe one building as "beautiful" and another as "ugly"—these are purely Western ways of thinking, although now as prevalent in Japan as in the West. Such thinking is the antithesis of *mu*, which sees beauty and ugliness as the same thing. But let us try to make the concept more concrete with examples, examples drawn from architecture rather than from ethics, the field more usually associated with *mu*.

At some unknown time in the distant past the Japanese builder began using a ruler called a *tawami-jaku* ("flexible rule"). This was used not for measuring length but for creating curves. The ruler, generally made from a thin strip of wood, could be of any length desired and its thickness could be varied, thicker in the middle, thicker at either or both ends, or of uniform thickness throughout. By applying pressure in varying degrees to the ends of this ruler the master carpenter could produce an infinite variety of curves, choosing from among them the one that best suited his immediate need for, say, upcurving eaves.

Rope or string also was used for creating curves. This method was called *nawa-darumi* ("slack rope"). For example, if the line of the eaves, particularly in the case of a thatched roof, is made geometrically straight, there is an optical illusion in which the roof seems to be sagging at either end. This can also be observed in the case of the roof ridge, though not to such a pronounced degree. To correct this illusion of sagging, the straight line was made into a long, almost imperceptible curve by the *nawa-darumi* method: the carpenter would draw a string taut, loosen it an inch or so, and follow the resulting curve in shaping eave line or roof ridge.

But note that these curves made by either the flexible rule or the slack string are derived in the first instance from a straight board to which man applies pressure and in the second from a string that begins as a straight line and is allowed to sag under the force of gravity. Hence, although the Japanese builder used both straight and curved lines, for him there was no basic opposition between the two categories as there is in the West, where undoubtedly the use of separate instruments (the straightedge for a straight line, compasses or the French curve for a curved line) underline the differences. Instead, the Japanese felt curves and straight lines to be identical. The flexible board or rope does not have a shape of its own but becomes either straight or curved only when man or nature applies force to it; both shapes

are created from the same instrument, from the same shapeless substance: are they not then identical? This phenomenon, incidentally, is also observed in the bamboo, so beloved by the Japanese, bent by a crown of snow: can one say the bamboo is either straight or curved? Is it not simply bamboo in the snow, the stuff of poetry and no less of architecture?

Leaving the field of architecture for the moment, we also find this same way of thinking at work in the traditional Japanese idea of beauty. A beautiful land, beautiful cities, beautiful buildings, beautiful gardens—yes, of course the Japanese wanted these as much as Westerners do. The difference was in how they set about achieving them. Certainly they would never have thought of speaking of "beauty for beauty's sake," nor of "changing ugliness into beauty." If all opposites are identical, then beauty cannot be approached by insisting upon the duality of beauty and ugliness, by seeking the one and avoiding the other. The substance of beauty cannot be achieved except through *mu*, through a denial of both ugliness *and* beauty or, to speak for a moment in terms of contemporary architecture, through a denial of both decoration *and* functionalism.

This was the point being made by the great tea-masters of the 15th and 16th centuries, who played such a large role in the development of Japanese aesthetics, when they gave high praise to folk wares. Beautiful as these wares certainly were, still they had been made by simple, innocent, nameless craftsmen and farmers without the slightest thought, or desire, to create "beauty." Were these not perfect examples of *mu*?

Similarly, no contradiction was found between new and old, luxurious and frugal, complicated and simple. Hence it is often difficult to detect a trend in the art and architecture of Japan's Middle Ages. On the one hand there was the increasing magnificence of much temple and mansion architecture, while on the other there was the austerity of the tea-ceremony room, nor was it considered the least unusual for such contrasts to be combined within a single architectural work. Here also is the explanation of the fact that so many temples, particularly of the Zen sect, looked more like ordinary homes. In Zen all things and all phenomena are alike expressions of Buddha: why then have special buildings for temples? The sound of the wind in pine trees or the roar of a waterfall—these were voices chanting the sutras; the shape of a mountain, of a tree, of a stone—these were images of the Buddha. Why should man compete with them? Four walls and a roof could make a temple, and an abstract garden could express all the truths of Zen. This was enough: all was one.

Surely such a philosophy could never comprehend the modern architect who strives to design a building completely different from those of his colleagues, who measures his success by his ability to free himself of any and all debt to tradition, who seeks in his own mind not simply to build a building worth the name but instead to create "beauty" or "functionalism." Instead, the Japanese builder relied heavily upon the great traditions of the past and yet was free to use these traditions in whatever new ways conditions demanded so long as he adhered, with pride, to the underlying order—he simply built his buildings as sincerely and truly as he could. So long as he followed the traditional system, order would be the result. So long as he believed firmly in the concept of *mu* and denied the duality of beauty and ugliness, beauty would result of itself. Certainly there were other ways of equal validity, but here was one tried and true way immediately at hand: why seek further?

And beauty he did achieve, beauty and order too. The photographs in this book attest to this. We have arranged the photographs and their accompanying commentary into the ten large categories that seem to us to have the most significance for today. Obviously such arbitrary categories are often overlapping, perhaps at times even self-contradicting. But some sort of classification is essential when approaching such a large subject, however indivisible it may seem.

Commentaries on the photographs themselves are gathered together at the back of the book, as we hope the reader will not follow them too closely, at least not until he has formed his own independent vision of the roots and contemporary meaning of Japanese architecture by absorbing the photographs into his own mind and heart. For ours is but one of many possible visions, and who can say which is the more valid? Certainly, whatever the viewer learns for himself directly from such inspiring examples of Japanese architecture will be worth much, much more than what he can gain from any number of inadequate words. By leaving the List of Plates, on the flap of the book's final leaf, folded out for quick reference as he goes through the book, he can keep himself roughly oriented, saving a reading of the commentaries for later.

If the concept of *mu* is difficult for us moderns to grasp, so is it likely to be with the underlying system and philosophy of any great architecture, especially of one embodying this same *mu*. But we are convinced the search is worth the effort: if the ancient Japanese discovered a way to architectural greatness through order and system, surely their example can be a guidepost for us as we seek, by different means, the same end.

I WOOD, STONE, EARTH

Out of their natural environment, from their long history, which are the building materials that the Japanese have chosen to favor above all others? In all lands the choice is of course largely determined by availability. And yet the question cannot be so simply answered. Even in countries with little to choose from but stone and wood we find the preference being given now to the one, now to the other. So, then, the final choice must be determined also partly by the requirements of social conditions and, perhaps even to a greater extent, partly by the inherent tastes formed in a people long before recorded history. Once the choice, for whatever reasons, has been made, it in turn becomes a determining factor in the future development of that people's architecture and way of life. Such has certainly been the case in Japan, where the building materials are of the simplest.

WOOD. First and foremost is wood. Japanese architecture is pre-eminently, almost exclusively, an architecture of wood. What clay was to the Babylonians or stone to the Greeks and Romans, so wood is to the Japanese, particularly in the favored forms of Japanese cypress and cryptomeria, and usually it is neither painted nor stained.

In primitive times the lordly tree was an object of deep religious veneration. Originally there were no shrine buildings in Japan. Instead, a tree, a forest, a giant boulder, or a mountain stood festooned with sacred ropes of worship. When the primitive Japanese first felled a tree and set it up as a center pillar for a shrine, this sacred quality followed it into their buildings. There the pillar towered, still dominating the space around it, and thus, for both religious and structural reasons, from the earliest days to the present it has been recognized as playing a guiding role in the establishing of architectural order.

Even today we see outstandingly majestic trees decorated with these same sacred Shinto festoons marking them as objects of veneration. Even today in rural Japan it is the central pillar of a house, the pillar upon which all the rest of the framework is structurally dependent, the pillar as essential to its structure as the keystone to the Roman arch, that is given the name *Daikoku-bashira,* "pillar of the God of Fortune." This is the pillar that is raised first, again to be decorated with the Shinto festoons, blessed by a Shinto priest, and offered prayers by the farmer and his family. Although much like roof-raising, cornerstone-laying, and other building ceremonies found the world over, this ritual of the central pillar somehow preserves a more deeply religious spirit. It is a significant token of the Japanese veneration for the tree both as one of nature's most awe-inspiring creations and as Japan's favorite building material.

The sacred tree dominated the space around it, inspiring veneration in the hearts of men. When it was brought to play a role in man's architecture, its space-dominating quality was retained. Hence the earliest Japanese uses of the pillar followed the pattern of nature, preserving the upright character of the natural tree and seeking too the tree's great majesty of height. Using architecturally primitive techniques, at the dawn of Japanese history master builders raised some of the greatest wooden buildings the world has ever seen. Though none of the buildings exist today, the magnificence of their conception remains on record as a landmark of architecture.

For example, there was the great East Pagoda of Todai-ji, the Nara temple of the Great Buddha. This pagoda, built in the year 764, had seven stories and rose to the amazing height of 312 feet. This statistic gains dramatic significance when we realize that it is the equivalent of a modern office building of more than thirty stories and

exceeds by more than three times the 101.7-foot limit set for buildings in Japan today. The pinnacle of the pagoda is said to have been hidden in the clouds.

As originally built, in 752, the hall housing the Great Buddha itself measured 282 by 166 feet, with a height of 146 feet, thus exceeding by 95 feet in length and 3.3 feet in height the present Great Hall, restored in 1914, even though this latter is itself reputed to be the largest wooden building in the world.

Legend gives the main structure at Izumo, the oldest shrine in Japan, a height of 174 feet, almost four times that of the present building.

But enough of measurements: those already given will indicate the tremendous scale of these ancient wooden buildings. Noble in concept though they were, due to the fact that they derived their principal method of construction from the natural tree itself—but without the tree's sturdy root system—they carried within themselves fatal structural flaws. Within twenty years after the completion of the Hall of the Great Buddha two pillars had to be added as extra supports for each of the original forty to keep the building from collapsing. And it is said that late one night the great shrine at Izumo crumbled to the ground without a sound. Man then completed the destruction of these great monuments, and the Todai-ji buildings disappeared forever in the flames set by Taira Shigehira on December 28, 1180, in his attack on the city of Nara.

And yet these very structural defects which, even leaving aside man's own destructive nature, foredoomed these buildings are at the same time a testimony to the ingenuity and ambition with which the ancient builders labored after their discovery of the pillar. For this reason these ancient buildings have long been eulogized as the first architectural masterpieces of Japan, as fitting monuments to the Japanese love of wood as a building material.

STONE.   After wood comes stone as the second most important building material. In the structure of buildings stones are actually used only for foundations, but ever since the 8th century their use for landscaping purposes has been so prevalent, and landscaping is so much an integral part of Japanese architecture, that it would be a serious mistake to overlook their important role. If Japan is a land of forests, it is also a land of rocks. There are the jagged crags of the deep mountains and the smooth, water-worn boulders of seaside and river bed; there are even the stones used to weigh down shingles in rural Nara Prefecture, poetically called "lingering snow." Yes, Japan is a land of rocks, and the Japanese have a deep reverence for them particularly in their natural shapes.

Man can shape stone, but in Japanese eyes nature is the greatest shaper of all, and the Japanese view is that nature's handiwork should be tampered with as little as possible, preferably not at all. Just as each human being has his own personality, so too does every rock and stone have a personality all its own; man's task is to perceive the personality of each stone, to understand the beauty of its own unique "wrinkles," and then to place the stone in such a way as to make the best use of its beauty and character.

In time this aesthetic of stones, this striving to find and make manifest beauties no one had previously perceived, was extended beyond the physical stones to include the entire garden landscape and even the man-made buildings. Thus stone has played a role in Japanese architecture far beyond its comparatively small use in foundations and landscaping.

17

EARTH.   And finally comes earth as the third most important building material. A comparative latecomer on the architectural scene, earth made its first, limited appearance in the 7th century in the form of the baked-clay roof tiles which, though never entirely supplanting thatch and bark shingles, have become such a prominent characteristic of later Japanese architecture. Only gradually and much later did earth gain the wider uses it came to have as a material for covering walls, making ovens and well curbs, bridges, garden enclosures, and the like. Originally the palaces, temples, and shrines had board walls, and earth was considered a building material fit only for peasants, its working even being relegated to one of the pariah castes. In the Middle Ages, however, the samurai and the townsman gradually adopted the material and raised it to a high art in the building of their castle walls, tea-ceremony rooms, and residences. Thus in later centuries earth, this basis of Japan's precious rice crop, came to play an equally important part in its architecture.

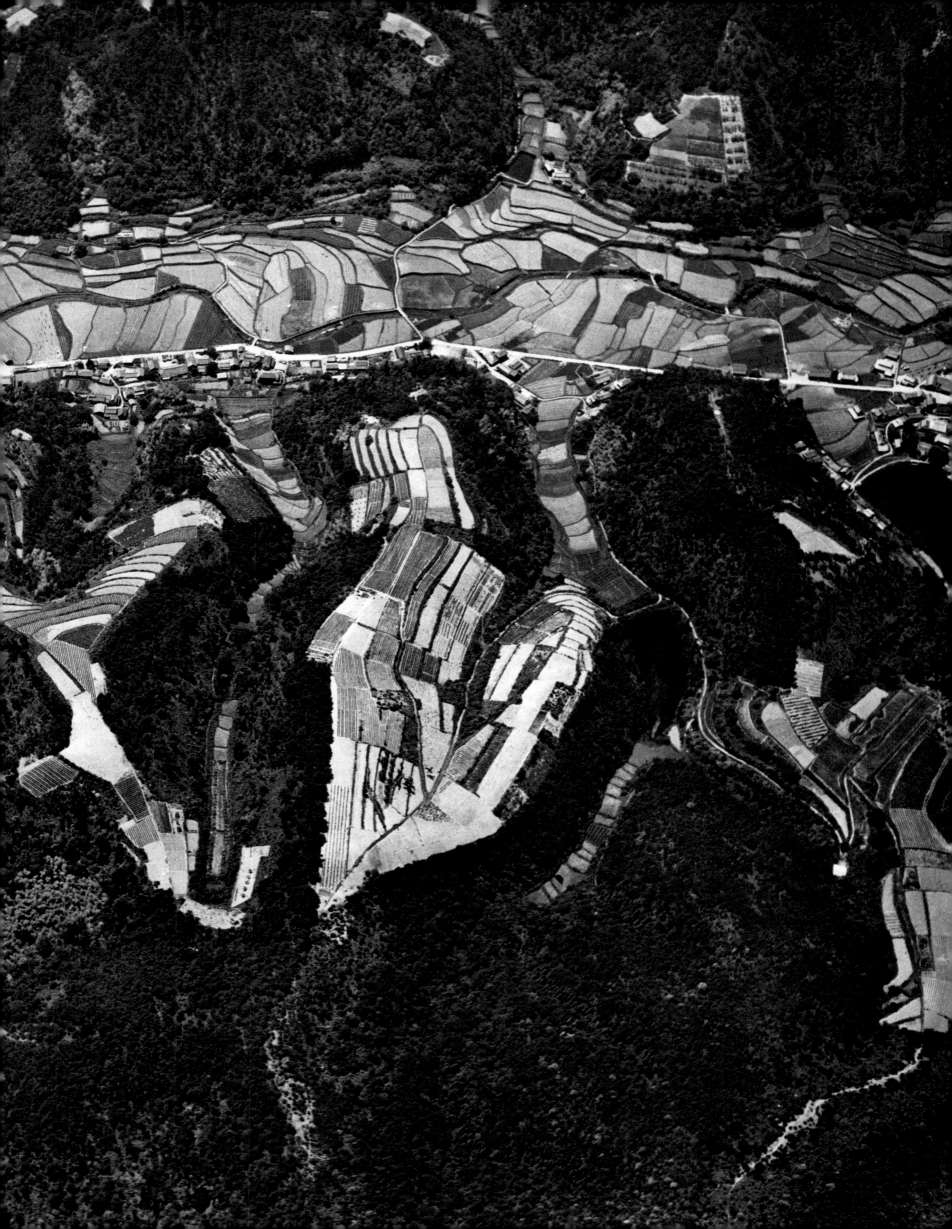

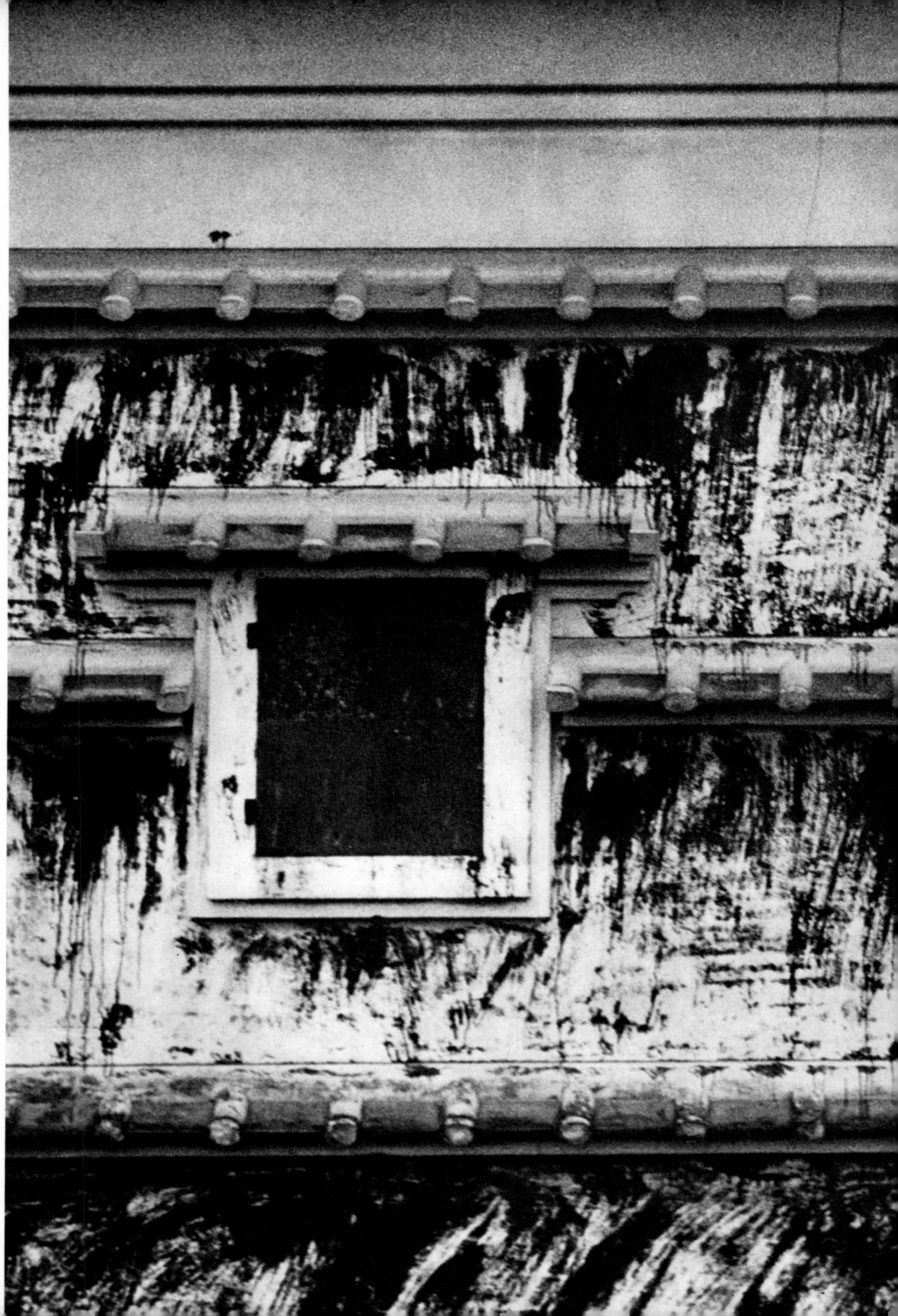

2 SETTING LIMITS TO INFINITY

Japanese religion began with the worship of objects of nature. Japanese architecture began when an enclosure was set up about a sacred, festooned tree, thus creating architectural space. The imperial ancestors, to honor the Sun Goddess at what is now the Grand Shrine of Ise, first claimed a small opening in the magnificent forest along the banks of the Isuzu River (see also Plate 2) and set up a fence around the clearing. The fence, the enclosure, set a limit to the infinity of the great unknown that faced primitive man and became thus a symbol of security and trust.

And yet, while these great enclosures from Japan's early history—those surrounding the grand shrines at Ise and Izumo, the temple cloisters of Horyu-ji, the mighty walls of Himeji Castle, the mud walls about the garden of the Katsura Imperial Villa —claimed bits of ground here and there from limitless infinity, at the same time they refused to admit that there ever could be a limit to the spaces they enclosed. This is the special characteristic of the Japanese enclosure: it sets a limit to infinity *on the outside*, and on the inside it re-creates a miniature universe, a new infinity, of its own.

30.

31.

3 DYNAMIC SPACE

As can be seen in such early examples as the temple complexes of Todai-ji and Horyu-ji, in the 6th to 8th centuries Japanese architecture was very much influenced by models from the Asiatic mainland—indeed, many of the builders themselves were brought to Japan from Korea—where the non-Japanese concept of social hierarchy had made dignity, austerity, and grandeur the goals of monumental architecture. Hence, like much of the traditional architecture of the West, in these early Japanese structures the spatial sequence, the distribution of parts, was rectilineal, grouped about an axis or axes of straight lines. One approaches these buildings and sees them geometrically arranged, one beyond the other or flanking the axis of approach at regular intervals. A natural result of this arrangement was the great emphasis placed upon the design of the facade.

In the 9th to 12th centuries, however, this rectilineal pattern was replaced by a concept more in keeping with Japanese thinking whereby architectural space was allowed to spread in indefinite extensions so long as a certain inner harmony was maintained. For one thing, the Chinese concept of hierarchy had proved antipathetic to the Japanese character. For another, in the rough terrain of Japan, especially in the mountains, where the esoteric sects of Buddhism preferred to build their temples and monasteries, and in the foothills about Kyoto, where the nobles were placing their villas, the rectilineal arrangement was both uneconomical and impractical, and its disregard of topography did not accord with the Japanese attitude toward nature.

The results of the new Japanese flexible arrangement of space were many. The stroll garden developed from the same concept, being designed so that a person could experience many different vistas as he strolled along its footpaths—pavilion, teahouse, viewing platform, pond, trees, stones, stone lanterns, a bridge, and always

the kaleidoscopic changing of the pattern of the buildings themselves seen now from this angle, now from that. Buildings could now be adapted to any terrain, even to the steep mountains of esoteric Buddhism.

Such an architectural complex as Horyu-ji was an organic whole in itself, a quiet body of perfection, whose harmony would be lost by the addition of a single further element; in short, this was a static balancing of space. Under the new arrangement, however, there was always the possibility of changing the organic whole by adding new elements, of adapting it to new functions and needs, of maintaining an inner

42

44

43

harmony even while absorbing new and often surprisingly disparate elements. In contrast with the older, the static, sequence of space, this was a sequence that can best be described as dynamic equilibrium.

This idea of freely permitting the absorption of varying spaces into an architectural whole, of permitting old and new elements to coexist harmoniously side by side, of constantly adapting to the needs of each new age, is surprisingly close to the spatial concepts of modern architecture of individual buildings and of city planning as well.

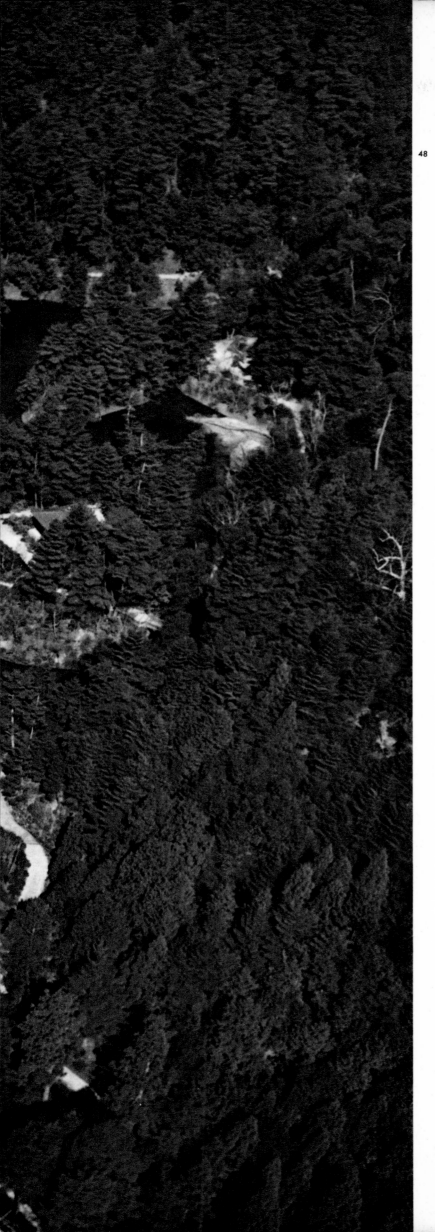

48

4 THE GARDEN AS A MINIATURE UNIVERSE

The Japanese garden is as much a part of architecture as are buildings themselves. Together garden and buildings constitute Japanese architectural space; separate them, and nothing remains but miscellaneous constructions. As discussed in Section 2, the enclosure sets a limit to infinity and creates a miniature universe of its own, but the bare enclosure has as yet no architectural significance. Landscape it, build within it, and architecture comes into being. To some extent the landscape and building designs determine the nature of the miniature universe that has been created by the enclosure. But it is a general principle of Japanese gardening that this created universe should never force its own image upon the viewer. It should be passive, unobtrusive, permitting all persons—of varying cultures, generations, sexes, and ages—to make their own interpretations of the miniature universe. This is not to say, of course, that a garden should be without character but rather that it should be profound enough in spiritual depth to admit of many interpretations.

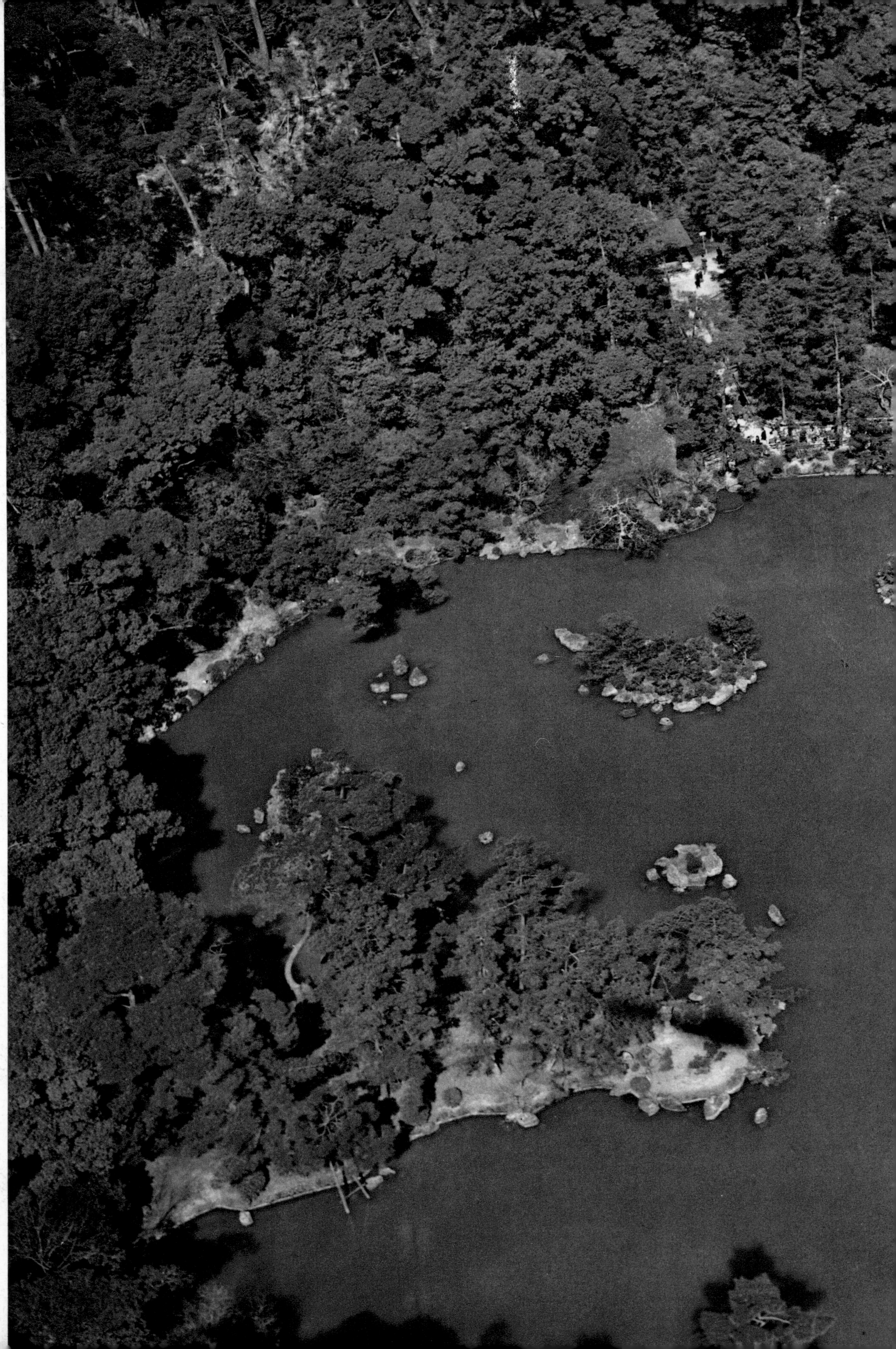

54

58

5 LINKING NATURE AND ARCHITECTURE

Magical in concept and execution though the miniature universe of the Japanese garden is, it would still have no place in the creation of architectural space were it not in some way made an integral part of the buildings it serves. One of the principal links between garden and house is the covered veranda, a prominent feature of Japanese architecture. Almost always floored with wood—though the straw mats of the house proper may occasionally spill over partially into it—the veranda may or may not be separated from the garden by sliding partitions. It functions both as a means of access to the rooms fronting it and as a means of regulating temperatures within the house, by obstructing the sun in summer and if, as is often the case, it has sliding doors at either edge, by providing air-space insulation in winter. Equally important as such practical considerations, however, is its very real aesthetic function of deepening the illusion of enclosed space by firmly linking together the otherwise disparate elements of house and garden.

6 THE PILLAR AND THE MAT

The modular concept of much contemporary architecture, like the resulting technique of prefabrication, is too familiar to require discussion. Nor is it needful here to go into the technical controversy that often engages architectural historians as to the exact role Japanese architecture played in this rather revolutionary development. However, a brief consideration of the traditional Japanese uses of the architectural module will serve the purpose of gaining a clearer insight into the basic principles of Japanese architecture.

The traditional Japanese carpenter needed neither sectional plans nor elevations for his work: a floor plan was sufficient. (Even today one can occasionally find carpenters working from nothing more than a floor plan sketched with bamboo pen and *sumi* ink on a thin board.) On this floor plan were indicated only the locations of the pillars, the nature of the partitions, and the code symbols showing how the various members of the structure's framework were to be fitted together. An understanding of the factors that make this possible will provide important clues to the Japanese conception of architectural space and methods of design.

Sectional plans and elevations were not needed for the simple reason that there had already been devised a definite system for the building of the framework. Hence, while the Japanese builder could no more ignore elevations and sections than can his Western counterpart, the existence of this system made possible the mental visualization of all parts beyond the floor plan. In other words, the measuring system had been standardized to the point of forming a complete vocabulary and grammar of building: follow the rules and a valid statement would result. It was simple as that.

Japanese construction methods may be roughly divided into two large categories, called *jikugumi* ("assembling the shafts") and *zosaku* ("fittings"). *Jikugumi* is the construction of the basic framework, the assembling of the pillars, beams, crossbeams, rails, etc., in short, the structuring of space. The resulting framework is the structural body, and once the positions of its pillars have been set, no further changes can be made without basic difficulties.

Zosaku, on the other hand, concerns everything after the basic framework—sliding doors, storm shutters, glass doors, walls, sills, headjambs, floors, alcoves, shelves —all those innumerable parts which, though essential for the finishing of a structure, can be more or less freely changed during or even after building. Note particularly that, unlike stone and brick construction, even walls are included in this second category, a fact that gives Japanese architecture a remarkable flexibility when it comes to the partitioning of space within the inflexible confines of the basic framework. True, certain walls have at times been assigned a more fundamental role in efforts to make Japanese houses more earthquake-proof, but traditionally all walls are considered as movable—or at least easily removable—partitions since they bear none of the weight of the roof.

In the setting up of the framework there are two different systems of measurement, that of the pillar, or *hashira,* and that of the straw mat, or *tatami,* which covers the floor.

The pillar system has been used from the earliest days to the present. Here the measurement of every member of the framework is defined as some proportion of the basic unit derived from the distance between the center of one pillar and the center of the next. This unit is generally called one *ken.* The *ken,* however, is a firm unit of measure only as applied to one particular structure; between one building and the next it may vary between 6 and 10 *shaku* (one *shaku* is only slightly shorter than one foot). For example, the *ken* of the earliest temples was generally about 10 *shaku,* whereas it had shrunk to about 7 *shaku* by the 11th century. Today there is also a *ken* that is an actual objective unit of measure, consisting always of 6 *shaku,* but the older variable *ken* of the carpenters is still to be found in a variance of almost 6 inches between that used in residential buildings of Kyoto and that of Tokyo. In short, in the pillar system, the size of the *tatami* was varied to suit whatever *ken* was used for a particular building and did not in itself provide a standard of measurement.

The *tatami* system came into general use in the 16th century with the increasing use of *tatami* in ordinary residences. Until that time the straw mat had been used only in the nature of a cushion in the homes of the upper classes, being placed wherever one sat; it was moved about at will, leaving the rest of the plank floors bare. As the *tatami* gained in popularity, however, it came to occupy more and more space until at last it covered the entire floor, thus leading directly to the development of the system of the *tatami* module.

In the *tatami* system the size of the mat provides the proportions for all other elements of a structure. Although there was, and still remains, some slight variation in the exact size of the *tatami* according to region and use, still the modular unit was now much more standardized in exact measurement than had been the variable *ken*. This all-important feature made possible for the first time the standardization of sizes of the fittings as well—in short, prefabrication, and in the 16th century!

Since the size of the mat was fixed (roughly at 3 by 6 feet), the inside measurement between two corner pillars likewise became fixed. But the distance between the centers of two pillars remained variable in accordance with the thickness of the pillars themselves, as well as with the size of the room.

These two systems—that of the pillar and that of the mat—have continued to exist side by side to the present day, with the preference decidedly going to the latter so far as domestic architecture is concerned. Traditionally, because of the variable *ken* of the pillar system and the variable measure between pillar centers in the *tatami* system, a separate set of measuring instruments was made for use in each building, and after the building was finished these measures were either preserved together with the plans or were placed in the hands of the owner. Today, however, still more standardization has become the general rule, and the ordinary carpenter working on the ordinary residence sometimes now relies on standard, store-bought measures, making necessary mental adjustments as he goes along. But it still is the system of the mat, or occasionally of the pillar, that he uses, and these two concomitants remain one of the most remarkable and fundamental characteristics of Japanese architecture.

76

7 OF TEA, BAMBOO, AND MORE PILLARS

Surprisingly enough, although the Japanese tea cult arose only in the 15th and 16th centuries, long after the pillar and *tatami* systems had seemingly established once and for all the basic patterns of Japanese architecture, this ceremonial drinking of tea not only quickly became a way of aesthetics for arts and crafts but was also to have a profound influence upon architecture.

There were originally two styles of teahouses. First there was the large, open, often beautifully decorated tearoom of the nobility. But it was the second style, the small, rustic room or house favored by the samurai and townsmen, that eventually won the day, extending its influence far beyond the confines of the teahouse itself to work significant changes in residential architecture as well.

The style that grew out of the teahouse is called *sukiya*, a term that has been variously interpreted. This style, or at least strong elements of it, is still much in evidence in residences and, particularly, in luxurious restaurants and inns. By following the teahouse's lead in pushing the pillars back into corners where they were partially hidden and no longer so much in the way, it greatly softened the structural rigidity of the pillar construction. By allowing the distribution of pillars without such geometrical attention to the roof structure, it permitted greater freedom in the planning and placement of interior partitions. The inside of a house could now be planned much more functionally, definitely a great step toward the modern theory of architecture. Even today many new houses in Japan still follow *sukiya* principles of design, precisely because of this functional quality.

In the *sukiya* style, then, the construction of the roof became more complicated since it had to adapt itself to the absence of pillars in the structurally most convenient places. As a result, wooden buildings could no longer be on such a large scale. On the other hand, irregularly shaped roofs permitted still greater freedom in fitting the structure to uneven terrain or oddly shaped building sites and resulted in much better utilization of land, a consideration of no mean importance in a land-hungry island nation.

In landscape art likewise, the tea ceremony played a large role, leading to the

development of the small, informal teahouse garden. Here steppingstones, which now form such a noticeable feature of Japanese gardens in general, first made their appearance. Although they had the functional use of providing clean access to the teahouse, their aesthetic function of informality and asymmetrical balance was given equal importance from the beginning.

The big influence of teahouse architecture is seen also in the introduction of new materials, such as bamboo, and in the increasing emphasis given to the design of such fittings as sliding doors and windows. The accompanying photographs, and many others in other sections of the book, speak for themselves concerning the great utility and beauty the Japanese found in bamboo, and the ingenuity of design they lavished upon sliding doors and windows.

And yet, for all these different patterns—the pillar system, the *tatami* system, the *sukiya* style, and myriad decorative details—Japanese architecture still remains an architecture of the pillar, and all the patterns have common advantages. First there is the quality of functionalism. The use of the pillar as the basic module has permitted Japanese architecture to change through the ages in such a way as to adapt itself to almost any requirements. The wooden buildings of Japan may often be destroyed by fire, earthquake, or flood, and they may also simply wear out, but almost never are they torn down the way modern office buildings are simply because they have outlived their usefulness.

The second great advantage lies in their extreme adaptability to Japanese living requirements. In a country of four distinct seasons, and for a people with a great love of the seasonal aspects of nature, the seasonal adaptability of the Japanese house is of prime importance—closed tight in winter with all its sliding doors, glass doors, and storm shutters; open to every breeze in summer; and accommodating itself with gradual and graceful changes to the coming of spring or of fall. The rooms themselves are similarly adaptable, as to both size and fittings, to the varying demands of life. Indeed this architecture of the pillar has important advantages, which we should consider well in devising our architecture of tomorrow.

84

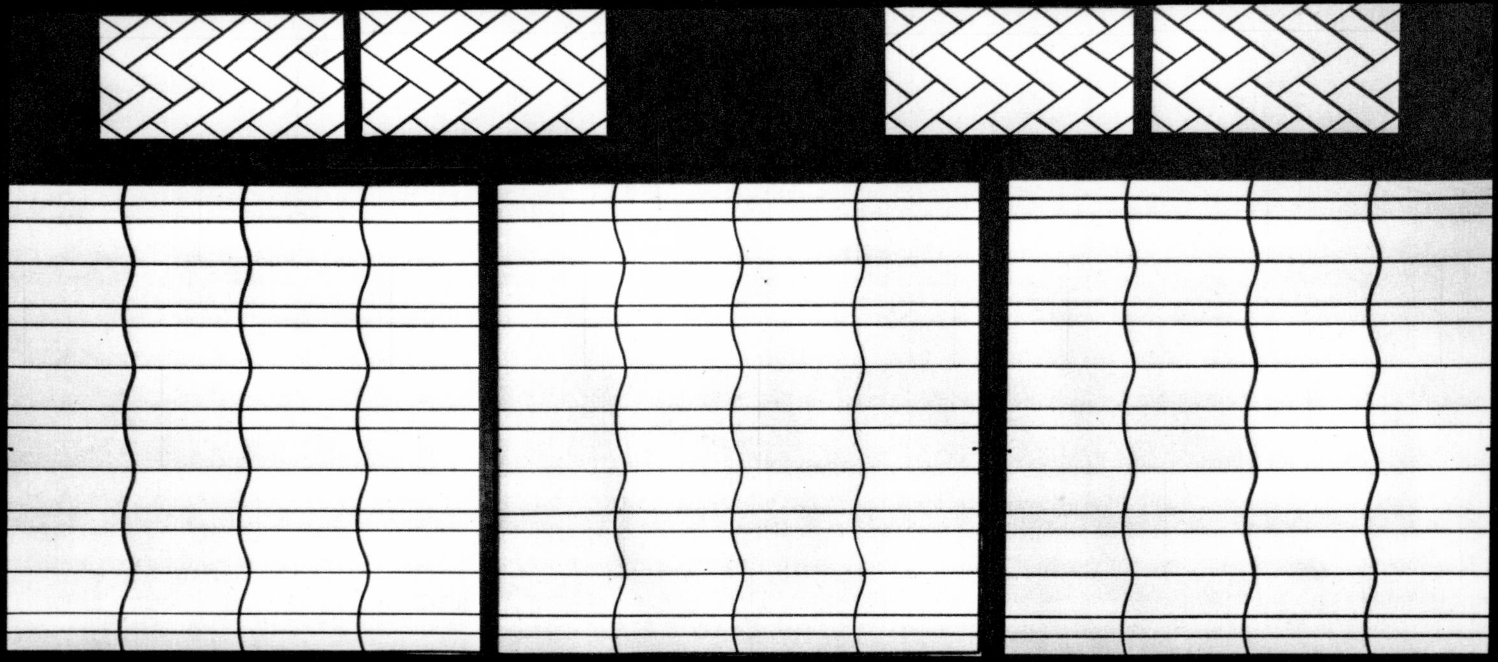

85

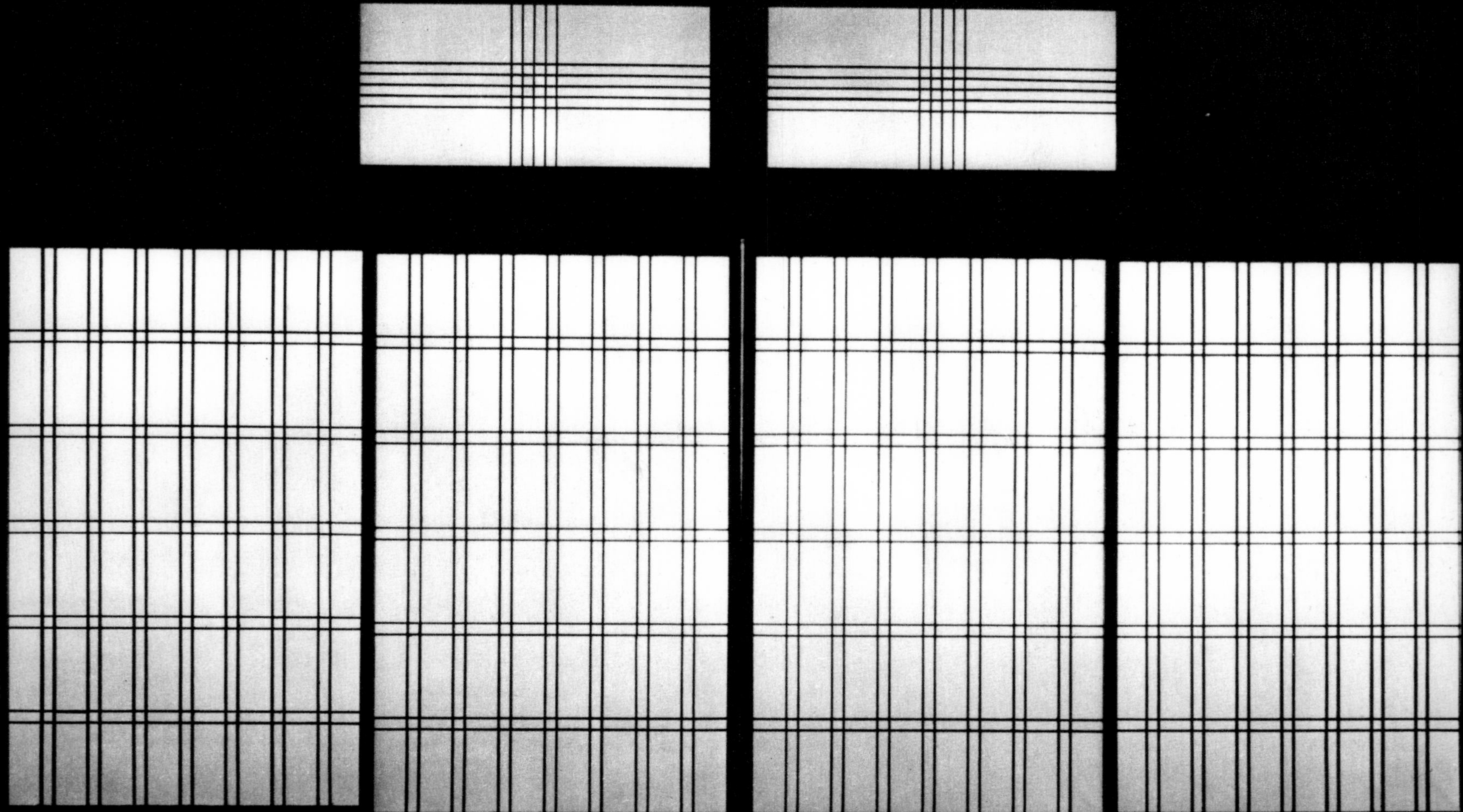

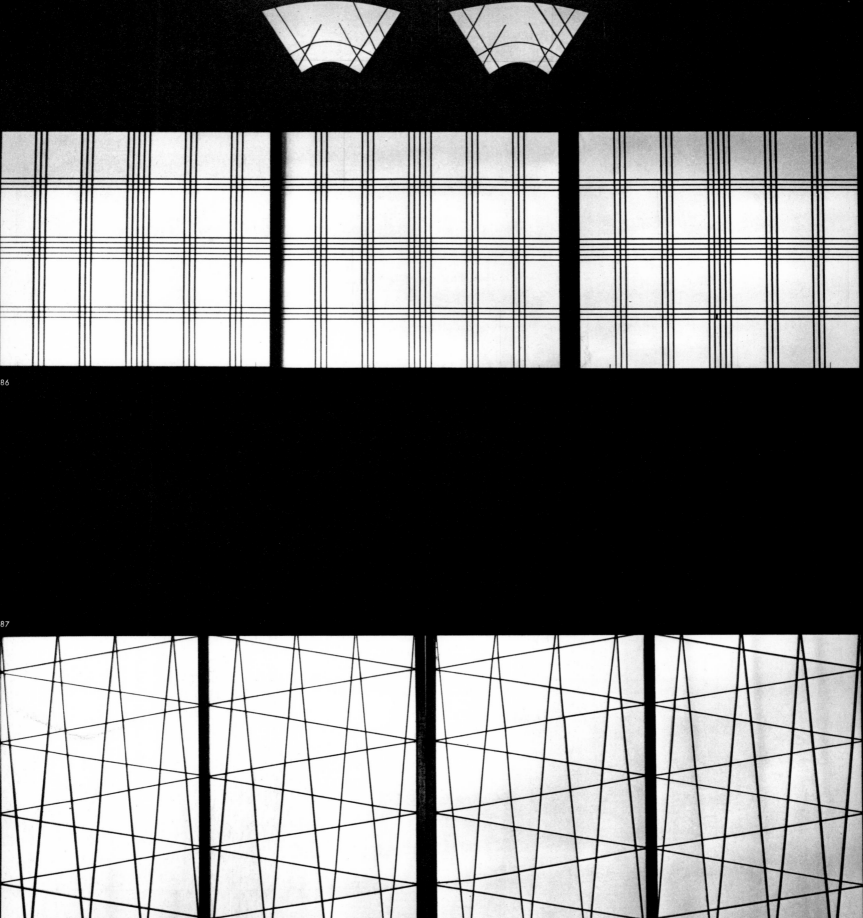

86

87

88

89

8 BORROWING SPACE

Of necessity the Japanese are a frugal people. Little wonder, then, that they have devised ways to make their buildings seem larger than they actually are: they "borrowed space" from the outside world and brought it into their homes, they absorbed nature itself into the miraculously plastic confines of man-made architectural space. In Section 4 we have already considered gardens as the settings for buildings; but there we were mainly concerned with looking from the garden toward the building and, in Section 5, with seeing how the two elements were fused together from an external point of view. Here, now, we turn our attention to the opposite point of view, looking at the garden from *inside* the building.

In some architectural styles, like that of the Grand Shrine of Ise, man-made architectural space is to be apprehended only from the outside, viewed like a piece of sculpture. In others, like those we are now considering, one goes inside the sculpture and, looking out, finds a magical new dimension of space, partly existing in nature but all undoubtedly man-made. Like the gardening principle of "borrowed landscape," here we have the architectural principle of "borrowed space."

Although the borrowed-landscape principle dates back many centuries, it was only slowly developed. Japan's oldest gardening manual, the *Sakuteiki*, written in

the 12th century, sets forth a somewhat contrary view when it says that the main object of landscaping is to comply with the will of nature. The borrowed-landscape principle is not stated and is only slightly foreshadowed when the author criticizes the garden design of the Toba Detached Palace for not having taken advantage of the natural beauty surrounding the site. The ancient capital cities of Nara and Kyoto had been built along Chinese geometrical street patterns in disregard of topography, thus giving slight opportunity for borrowed landscape. Hence it was only with the development of the more flexible style of construction that the borrowed landscape came into wide use. As the nobles of Kyoto moved out of the flat, regularly laid-out city into the surrounding foothills, their houses underwent corresponding changes in style, and by the 15th century we find the principle of borrowed landscape in full flower. It was a principle that was to give both Japanese landscape and architecture one of their most characteristic aspects. For it was only a slight step—but a mighty one—to say that if natural landscape could be borrowed and brought into the garden, so could natural space be borrowed and brought into the house. Yes, the homes of Japan are truly wide and spacious—not in physical measure, certainly, but as airy dwellings for the spirit.

9 RHYTHMS OF THE VERTICAL PLANE

Speaking of Japanese architecture in musical terms, the pillars are the score and, when joined with the other members that comprise the basic framework, determine the rhythm of the composition. This basic rhythm is then given its texture and embellishments by the additions of the vertical planes of walls, windows, sliding doors, shutters, and the like. Thus is the structure completed. And sometimes it is a composition as complex as a Mondriaan painting and at other times it is a quiet repetition of a single theme in many subtle modulations. And always, because of the deep overhang of the eaves, there is the beauty of dark shadows to create an ever-changing counterpoint of light and shade against the vertical planes of the finished building.

The architecture of the modules of pillar and mat, the *sukiya* style, the dynamic sequence of space, the variable *ken* measure—all these are behind us. Now we turn to the actual composition itself, the subjective, visual, musical beauty of the house as a whole.

102

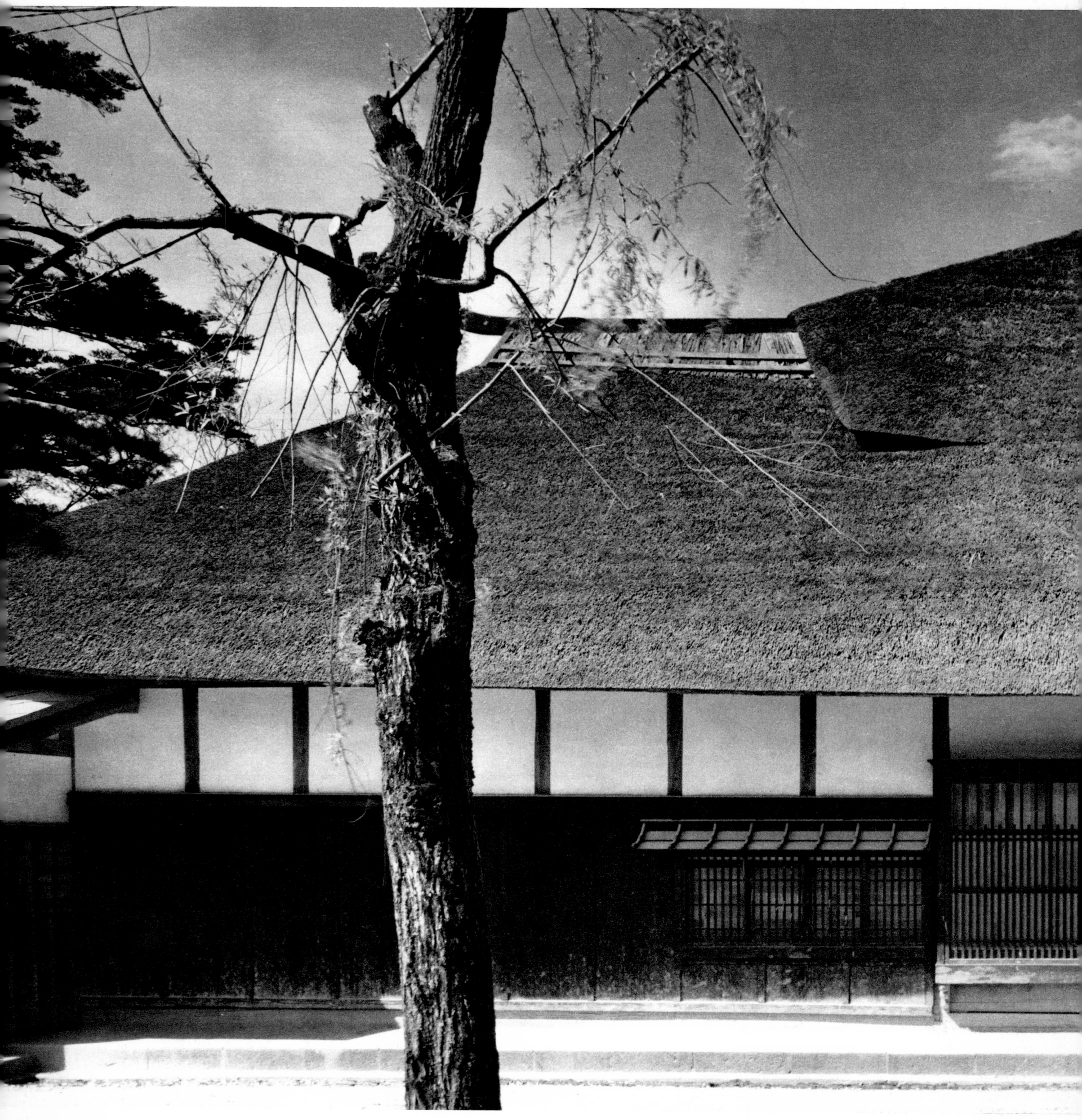

IO THE ROOF AS SYMBOL

And, finally, there is the roof, a striking feature of Japanese architecture both because of its physical prominence and its symbolic connotations.

In a country of earthquakes one would have thought the roofs would have been kept as light as possible. That, however, is far from being the case in Japan, where a large, heavy roof with deeply overhanging eaves is one of the most prominent characteristics of the architecture. There are a number of reasons for this. First, the pillar method of construction already provided more protection against earthquakes than do buildings of brick and stone. Second, in a land of much climatic variation wide eaves were very desirable, when combined with a southern exposure, in order to keep out the summer sun and bring in the sunlight in winter. Third, extended eaves also served to keep out the rain during the wet season. Lastly, since wooden architecture is always prone to rot, a solid, leakproof roof was essential.

But leaving such practical considerations aside, the Japanese roof also came to have a deeply symbolic value. It was the greatest challenge to the craft-proud builder and hence the part of the building on which he lavished the most care, particularly so in the case of the great monumental structures. Approached from a distance, the roof was the first part to come into view and established, as it were, the character of the building from afar, the skyward-pointing pinnacle of a pagoda reminding man of deity and the awe-inspiring roof layers of a castle-keep speaking

114

to him of authority. The same roofs also became familiar and beloved landmarks. As the proudest part of a building, the most readily visible part, the roof thus acquired a mystique of its own.

A status symbol? Yes, certainly, it was that too. What farmer would not feel the taller to see some of the rural roofs pictured here and be able to say that that was his, that it had been his father's and grandfather's and would be his son's and grandson's? But it was more than mere status, much more. Whether of temple or farmhouse, the roof was a link between heaven and earth. It pulled toward the sky, and yet remained firmly set on beams, beams on pillars, pillars on foundation stones, all firmly anchored to the earth that gives us rice and life, and yet all lifting that soaring roof high above the earth toward the heavens that give us aspirations beyond life.

Rhetoric? Yes, but during the centuries in which traditional Japanese architecture was a living, growing thing, this symbol of the roof as a link between heaven and earth was a consciously recognized reality for the Japanese of those days. Today, with the world much smaller and with the beginnings of a new architectural tradition that would transcend all national boundaries, we must find equally valid symbols. If this quest for the roots of the old Japanese architecture can be of any help in pointing the way, it is a gift gladly given.

COMMENTARIES ON THE PLATES

1. *Cryptomeria tree. Kasuga Shine precincts, Nara.* It was the cryptomeria, lord of the Japanese forest, standing in noble majesty, that was often religiously revered by the ancient Japanese, that became in a sense one of his favorite spiritual symbols. And at the same time this high-reaching, straight-growing tree served as an inspiration for those early builders who first discovered the principle of the pillar. Appropriately, then, the cryptomeria, also called *sugi* or Japan cedar, provides one of the most favored Japanese building materials. Similarly favored is *hinoki* or Japanese cypress.

2. *Inner Precincts, Grand Shrine of Ise, Mie Prefecture; reconstruction of 3rd(?)-century original.* Dedicated to the Sun Goddess, legendary ancestor of the Japanese imperial family, and housing the mirror that forms one of Japan's three sacred treasures, this is probably the best remaining example of purely Japanese architecture as yet without any Chinese influences. Although believed to have been established later than the Izumo Shrine, the latter is now so altered in appearance that the Ise Shrine can be taken as the starting point of Japanese architecture. Although the buildings have been reconstructed about every twenty years, at least since the first recorded reconstruction in 685 (note in the photograph the empty enclosure awaiting the next reconstruction), the original style has been faithfully preserved. The physical location of the shrine also gives a good idea of another principle of Japanese architecture, that of adapting itself to its natural surroundings rather than attempting to dominate them.

3. *Tumulus of Emperor Nintoku, Osaka; 5th century.* This is the largest of Japan's imperial mausoleums, measuring 1,558 by 984 feet and surrounded by three concentric moats. Constructed just prior to the architectural epoch that saw the great wooden building replace the tumulus as the imposing, monumental structure, this was the largest man-made structure in Japan at the time. Next were to come, first, in the late 5th century, the palace, symbol of imperial authority and power, and then,

about two centuries later, the Buddhist temple, symbol of religious authority and of architectural debt to China, to supplant the tumulus as Japan's monumental structures.

4. *Farmhouses, Kazura Village, Gifu Prefecture; 18th-19th centuries.* This is a farm village deep in the mountains and serves us here as a symbol for one of the two great lineages of Japanese architecture. The first is that of shrines, temples, palaces, and mansions; the other, shown here, is that of the ordinary residence, the homes of Japan's farmers, merchants, townsmen, petty samurai, and the like. In an agricultural nation, such as Japan primarily was until the present century, is not the farmhouse the most representative example of this residential architecture? Though naturally disdained by nobles, warriors, and townsmen alike, the farmhouse was to have a strong influence upon the residences of the upper classes in the Middle Ages, when they copied the teahouse, which in many ways was but a refinement of the farmhouse style.

WOOD, STONE, EARTH

5. *Grain of wood.* Not only is wood the most favored building material in Japan, but the Japanese also have a deep love for its unadorned textures. The precious woods used, for example, for the ornamental post of the alcove of a house's principal room are often left with the bark still on and almost never is the grain of the wood concealed with paint.

6. *Isuzu River, Grand Shrine of Ise, Mie Prefecture.* This beautiful river flowing through the shrine precincts is as much a part of the shrine as are the buildings themselves. Here worshipers wash their hands and rinse their mouths before proceeding to the shrine proper. The pillar in the foreground is set up to protect the piers of a bridge in times of flood. As in all Shinto architecture, designed on the principle that any decoration would conceal the essential substance of the construction itself,

124 ▶

there is nothing here but the utmost simplicity, the absence of all flourish, the love of wood in and for itself.

7. *Inner Precincts, Grand Shrine of Ise, Mie Prefecture; reconstruction of 3rd(?)-century original.* Again the lordly cryptomeria and, in the background, a view of the native Japanese architecture that it inspired. The posts of both building and fence are set into the ground in primitive style, one reason why the shrine needs periodical rebuilding. The thatched roofs too need replacing frequently. Only the feeling of the structures is old—coeval, one almost feels, with the surrounding trees and boulders and the crystal flow of the Isuzu River nearby. The billet-shaped objects on the roof ridge, called *katsuogi*, served to give added weight to the roof as protection against typhoons. Although their functional use has since been lost, *katsuogi* are still frequently found as decorations on Shinto roofs.

8. *Gatepost, Great South Gate, Todai-ji, Nara; 1199.* Sturdy as the tree from which it came, this giant post, measuring 63 feet in height and 3.2 feet in diameter, has been standing here for over seven hundred years. In the background are visible the low roof of the Middle Gate and the high roof of the Great Hall.

9-10. *Shoso-in treasure house, Todai-ji, Nara; late 8th century.* Although not of such gigantic scale as the original Great Hall and East Pagoda of Todai-ji, this treasure house, with all its contents (property of the Emperor Temmu), has fortunately withstood the ravages of time and man's destructiveness. Like many other storehouses of the period, this was built in the manner of a log cabin. The logs swell in the wet season and thus keep out the damp; then in the dry season they contract, opening cracks for ventilation; whether deliberately or by chance, this method of construction is responsible in large part for the excellent state of preservation of the contents. The building rests on 40 pillars, each measuring 2.3 feet in diameter.

11. *Fence in Inner Precincts, Grand Shrine of Ise, Mie*

Prefecture; reconstruction of 3rd(?)-century original. Like the shrine buildings themselves, the fences are rebuilt every twenty years in their original style. The method of burying the posts in the ground is indeed primitive, but in its shape, perfect proportions, and veneration of wood as a building material this fence is a work of art.

12. *Grand Shrine of Izumo, Shimane Prefecture; 18th-century reduced-scale reconstruction in traditional primitive style.* This reconstruction is only 43 feet high as against the 174 feet which legend gives the original structure, believed to have predated even the Ise Shrine. The primitive building, of such staggering height, is said to have rested on pillars made by binding three huge pieces of wood together with iron bands. In form the original building is said to have followed that of the imperial palace in use at the time when the chieftain ruling this part of Japan placed his lands under the imperial dominion and raised this shrine in token of fealty. Hence, even though the present structure has been considerably changed in shape, perhaps it still echoes the native Japanese palace style of architecture at the time when the great palaces replaced the imperial tumuli as monumental structures.

13. *Eave bracketing, Kyoto Imperial Palace; 1855 reconstruction of late-8th-century original.* Although destroyed by fire several times—twice in recent centuries alone—this palace has been rebuilt each time on the previous model and hence retains much of the style of the original buildings as raised by the Emperor Kammu in 794. Even so, certain of its details, such as the treatment of the eave bracketing, show undoubted Sino-Buddhist influences. But its air of refined simplicity and its emphasis upon the inherent beauty of unadorned wood remain uniquely Japanese.

14. *Country merchant's house (Kusakabe residence), Gifu Prefecture; 19th century.* Here we turn from temples and palaces to the ordinary residence to see the use of wood in the second great division

of Japanese architecture. This is the residence of a country merchant. The room beyond the sliding doors is used for both living and dining, while the smaller rooms at the right are for the reception of business clients. The architectural pattern of pillars, beams, and sliding partitions, with the emphasis always on wood, is indeed a thing of great beauty.

15. *Farmhouse (Takano residence), Yamanashi Prefecture; 18th century.* Here we look into the attic of a large old farmhouse to observe the uppermost thrust of the structure's great central pillar, crudely shaped from a giant of a tree. Farmhouse attics such as this are usually used for the raising of silkworms; this particular one, however, is used for the drying of licorice.

16. *Sea-worn boulders, Kagoshima Prefecture.* In Japan's long art history there have been famous artists who have devoted their careers to the painting of natural stones such as those seen here or those found in the deep mountains. Fabulous prices are often paid for a stone with just the right "personality" for its intended use, and such stones are transported as carefully as eggs to preserve their original moss, their natural patinas.

17. *Garden stone, Ryuko-in priests' quarters, Daitoku-ji, Kyoto.* Just an ordinary stone such as might be found almost anywhere in Japan, set in a bed of gravel. This is one of the "secrets" of Japanese landscape art: to create a new and living environment by giving ordinary stones the space and setting in which to express their personalities.

18. *Rock garden, Ryoan-ji, Kyoto; attributed to Soami (1472–1523).* This is one of the most famous gardens in all Japan. It is composed of fifteen rocks, sparse patches of moss, and gravel raked in patterns. Many persons say they cannot understand this garden, but nevertheless their hearts seem drawn to it. Rather than an abstract work of art, it is a symbol of Zen philosophy and contemplation. But beyond all such considerations it was and remains a profound expression of the Japanese love of natural stone for its own sake and the desire to give stones an environment that will enhance their beauty.

19-20. *Steppingstones, Heian Jingu shrine, Kyoto; late 19th century.* As these two views of steppingstones across a pond show, when it is found necessary to shape stone, the Japanese prefer the simpler shapes and always try to keep the shaping to a minimum. The irregular placement of the steppingstones also is characteristic.

21. *Castle wall and moat, Himeji, Hyogo Prefecture; 16th-17th centuries.* The wall is made, without mortar, of natural and roughly shaped stones and surmounted by a plastered, roofed parapet studded with loopholes. The haphazard pattern of light and shade made by the gaps between the irregularly shaped stones is a fortuitous by-product of the battlement's functional purpose. In China such a wall would have been built of brick, but the Japanese always preferred stone.

22. *Temple stairway, Jingo-ji, Kyoto; 12th century.* This approach to the main gate of the temple is made of natural stones which have been only slightly shaped on their tops to produce roughly flat treads. Unpretentious and unstudied as the stairway may appear at first glance, it is safe to say that this is exactly the effect carefully sought by the builders.

23. *Windbreak, Sotodomari Village, Ehime Prefecture; 19th century.* Built over a hundred years ago, not by professional stonemasons but by the local fishermen-farmers of this typhoon-ravaged coast, this windbreak of unmortared natural stones seems practically a product of nature.

24. *Rice paddies, Noto Peninsula, Ishikawa Prefecture.* In the construction of the all-important rice paddy, the source of the nation's staple food, earth has played a vital role since the dawn of Japan's history.

25. *Farm fields, an island in the Inland Sea, Hiroshima Prefecture.* A people who could work as artistically and functionally as this in earth were sure one day

to bring this same skill to apply to their architecture.

26. *Storehouse, Muroto Village, Kochi Prefecture.* For the purpose of fire prevention, the wooden walls of this storehouse have been plastered with mud and then finished with white plaster. The black smears are the remains of a wartime effort at camouflage against bombing raids. At first glance structures such as this would seem to follow the wall-construction methods of the West, but underneath the plaster there is the same Japanese-style framework, with the roof supported by pillars and not by the walls.

27-28. *Temple roofs, Toshodai-ji, Nara; 8th century.* Introduced by builders from Korea and China, since the 7th century the undulating swirls of the tile roof have been one of the noteworthy features of Japanese architecture; with them, earth as a building material had come into its own in Japan. Here the muted grays of the tiles are beautifully set off by the golden ornaments at the peaks.

29. *Storehouse, Koyama residence, Okayama Prefecture; 19th century.* Formerly a storehouse for fish, this unusual building is today an archaeological museum. Covered almost entirely with earth-derived materials, it has a tile roof and its walls also are faced with flat tiles set into white plaster.

SETTING LIMITS TO INFINITY

30-31. *Inner Precincts, Grand Shrine of Ise, Mie Prefecture; reconstruction of 3rd(?)-century original.* Two views of the enclosure of the inner shrine. Note the fences within fences.

32. *Grand Shrine of Izumo, Shimane Prefecture; 18th-century reduced-scale reconstruction in traditional primitive style.* There is but a single fence about this sacred enclosure, but it serves the same purpose as do the multiple fences of Ise, to set a limit between the mundane world and the world of divinity.

33-34. *Himeji Castle, Hyogo Prefecture; 16th-17th*

126

centuries. The castle is set on a hill and its multiple walls follow the contours of the terrain. Here the purpose of the enclosure is again to set a limit, not between the mundane and the divine but between safety and danger.

35-36. Horyu-ji, Nara Prefecture; 7th century and later. This temple complex contains some of the oldest wooden structures still standing in the world. The covered galleries that fill out the four sides of the enclosure form a sort of latticework cloister that permits one to see into the enclosure. Again the purpose is to keep out the mundane world. And again the result is the creation of a new universe in miniature within the enclosure.

DYNAMIC SPACE

37. Garden entrance, Katsura Imperial Villa, Kyoto; 17th century. An excellent example of the dynamic concept of architectural space, here stepping-stones form the footpath leading, without pretentious regularity, to the garden, branching away from the approach to the villa's main entrance. The eye is presented with no balanced symmetry, no imposing facade; instead, there is a tempting invitation to stroll up the easy slope and to see the whole view of the garden gradually open.

38. Temple approach, Horyu-ji, Nara Prefecture; 7th century. Here the static, rectilineal concept of the earliest Japanese temple architecture is seen both in its perfection and in its limitations. The straight, tree-lined road (not the automobile road to the left of it, which is a modern addition) leads with geometric precision to the Great South Gate, beyond which the buildings for priests' quarters stand foursquarely on either side of the wide, straight path, which leads on, through the Middle Gate, to the geometrically arranged cloister complex containing the various halls of worship—all precisely placed on an exact axis, all forming a perfect whole of quiet grandeur which would be irreparably harmed by the addition of a single extraneous element.

193

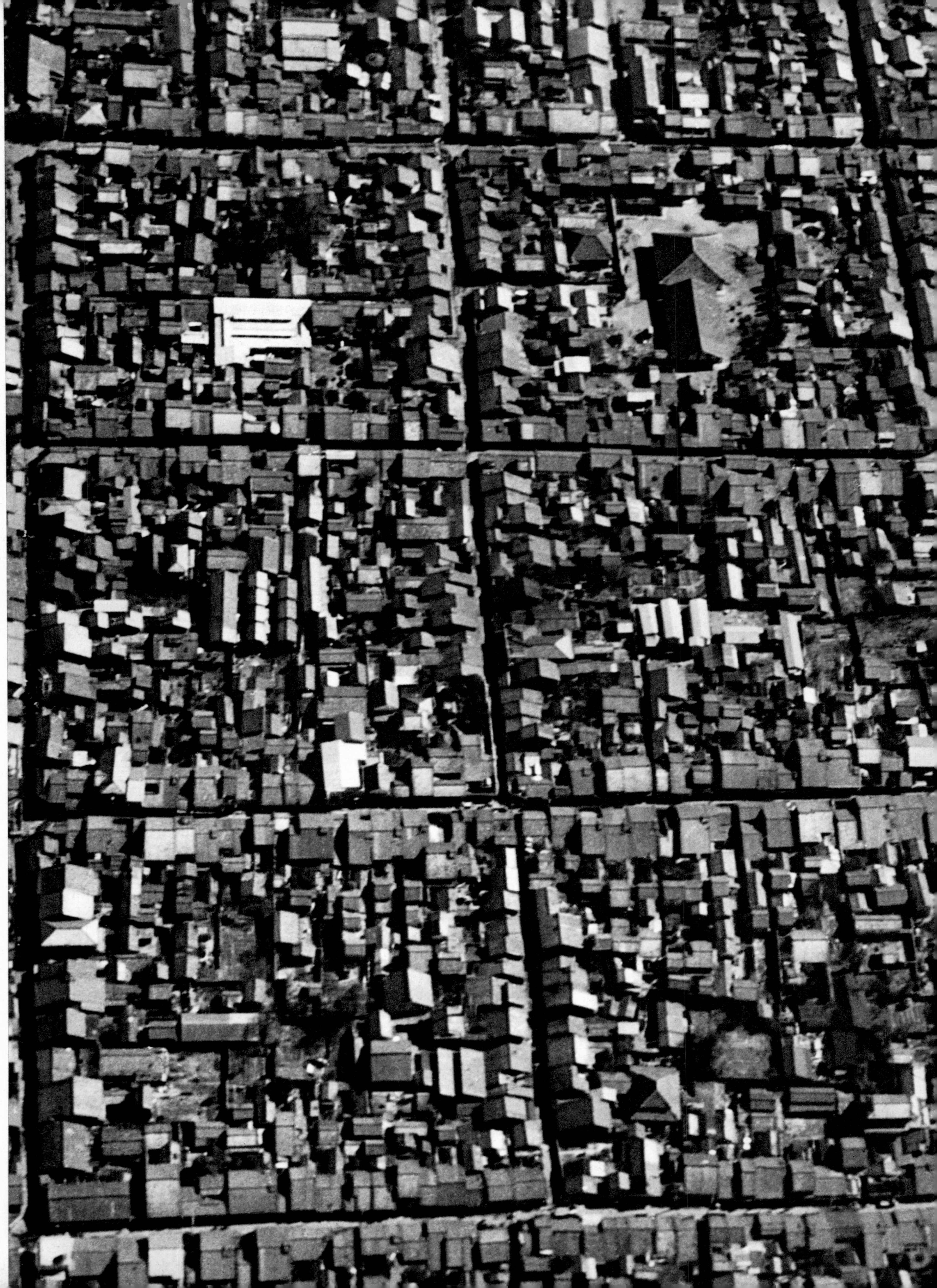

39-41. *Temple approach, Todai-ji, Nara; late-12th-and early-18th-century reconstruction of 8th-century original*. Although destroyed and rebuilt twice, the Todai-ji temple complex still retains its original rectilineal style. This spread of three photographs allows the viewer to imagine himself walking slowly toward the temple's Great South Gate. First the gate appears between the rows of pine trees. Gradually the Middle Gate too becomes visible, and finally the soaring roof of the main hall of worship with golden ornaments at the peaks. Thus the eye, and the mind, is led always onward in a straight line to the innermost precincts, to be met finally by the imposing majesty of the main hall's facade. It is a geometric journey of grandeur and perfection, but more Chinese than Japanese in concept.

42-43. *Ginkaku-ji (Silver Pavilion), Kyoto; 1479*. How different in spirit is the dynamic spatial concept of this temple from the rectilineal arrangement seen in the preceding plates! Originally a nobleman's villa, the Silver Pavilion (oddly enough, the pavilion of the complex was never actually covered with silver leaf as originally intended, but the popular name still persists) was made into a temple after his death. Its spatial sequence is a model of flexibility. One enters by the small gate at the lower right of Plate 43, immediately turns right and walks up the long, hedge-bordered walk of Plate 42, turns left through a second gate into a small compound from which one can either enter the building itself or proceed on to yet a third gate, which opens onto the spacious stroll garden seen at the upper left of Plate 43. The garden itself, attributed to Soami, is a work of surpassing art and plays an important role in the dynamic-space quality of the entire complex.

44-47. *Teigyoku-ken teahouse, Shinju-an priests' quarters, Daitoku-ji, Kyoto; 15th century*. In the architecture of the tea cult, developed in the 15th and 16th centuries, we find the ultimate development of the asymmetrical, dynamic sequence of space. The sequence of four photographs gives a good idea of the changes in space one encounters in approaching and entering this teahouse famed as the one-time residence of the Zen priest Ikkyu (1394-1481). In Plate 44 the teahouse itself is only gradually visible as one approaches over the steppingstones through the small entry garden. The doorway (Plate 45) is intentionally kept so low that the visitor, of whatever rank, must stoop to pass through to participate in the democracy of the tea ritual, and also to emphasize the smallness, remoteness and otherworld quality of the tearoom beyond. Plate 46 shows the tiny entryway with the steppingstones still continuing, thus not quite yet severing one's connection with the outside world; the stones lead first to the stone basin for rinsing the hands and then on into the teahouse proper, the tearoom of which is seen in Plate 47. This room consists of but three straw mats in area, with a charcoal hearth for the heating of the tea water cut out in the corner of one of the mats. The walls are of unfinished mud plaster and the ceiling of bamboo, both refined variations of the peasant-house style. A tiny garden is visible from the tearoom when the paper-covered windows are slid open, but the very fact that only a portion of the garden can be seen from any one position gives it the illusion of being surprisingly large.

THE GARDEN AS A MINIATURE UNIVERSE

48. *Stroll garden, Shugakuin Imperial Villa, Kyoto; 17th century*. Located in the foothills north of Kyoto, the site of this magnificent garden for an imperial villa commands a fine view of mountains and farmland. These natural views are deliberately utilized to blend and form a contrast with the garden area itself, thus producing the kind of garden known as a *shakkei*, a "borrowed landscape." Within the garden a network of footpaths weaves in and out among the ponds, copses, hillocks, grassy plots, and the three main summerhouses that are scattered about the grounds.

49-50. *Reflecting pool, Phoenix Hall, Byodo-in, near Kyoto; early 11th century*. Originally the country villa of a nobleman, in 1052 this was made a Buddhist temple by his son. The interior of the hall, which is itself one of the jewels of Japanese architecture, is decorated to give an illusion of paradise, while the reflecting pool in front and the natural setting at the back reinforce the sense of separation from the mundane world. Built to represent a phoenix in flight, the two wings are raised off the ground by pillars and when seen reflected in the water do seem magically suspended in air.

51. *Reflecting pool, Joruri-ji, near Kyoto; 12th century.* The garden and pool seem untouched by man, and even the low sweep of the temple seems almost a part of nature too. This is a magic universe created by a people whose religious inspiration has always begun with nature.

52. *Stroll garden, Kinkaku-ji (Golden Pavilion), Kyoto; 1394.* Again a stroll garden around a residential-style Zen temple that was originally a nobleman's villa. The pavilion itself was burned down in 1950 by a young lunatic priest who, in Yukio Mishima's novelized version of the tragedy, *The Temple of the Golden Pavilion*, became obsessed with the building as a symbol of beauty. The modern reconstruction is still garish with its gold-leaf covering, but in a few centuries, with the soft patina of time which the original possessed, it too will doubtless again create a beautiful, quiet contrast with the green of the vegetation, especially when reflected in the pond. From the viewpoint of Japanese architecture, there is always ample time, and centuries are not too much to wait for the creation of even a miniature universe.

53-54. *Stroll garden and meditation garden, Saiho-ji (Moss Temple), Kyoto; attributed to the Zen priest Muso Kokushi (1275-1351).* This out-of-the-way garden is made up of two distinct parts. In Plate 53 is a small portion of the stroll garden, in which a quiet pond is surrounded by footpaths heavily shaded by trees and bordered with deep growths of some fifty varieties of moss. The moss-grown stones, seemingly arranged so negligently, are deliber-

ately placed so as to present the strolling viewer with constantly changing patterns of symbolic significance. Plate 54 shows a corner of the garden of meditation, meant to be enjoyed by an observer seated in one of the vantage points. This is one of the oldest rock gardens in Japan and has had a great influence upon landscape art.

55-56. *Stone garden, Ryoan-ji, Kyoto; attributed to Soami (1472-1523). (See also Plate 18.)* Another garden for meditation, comprised of but rocks, raked gravel, and moss. This type of garden, called *kara-sansui* or "dry landscape," was originally devised for sites where water was unavailable. The style subsequently became popular as a means of symbolizing the philosophical concepts of Zen Buddhism, and today it is often used for the creation of gardens in abstract style. But first and always this garden is a moving example of the principle that the garden should not shout but instead should lie passive, awaiting the interpretation of its viewers. Surely the Ryoan-ji garden has had more interpretations than almost any other, and who is to say which is right? Is it not enough that one, even while saying he doesn't understand, never tires of looking at it? This is the ideal of Japanese landscape art.

57. *Garden detail, Sampo-in, Kyoto; 19th century.* Although only a tiny corner of a large, elegant stroll garden, does this not manage to create a world of its own? It is made of nothing more than carefully shaped patches of moss set in a bed of pebbles. It was deliberately made to be unobtrusive so as not to disrupt the harmony of the large, 16th-century garden of which it is a part.

58. *Raked sand in garden, Ginkaku-ji (Silver Pavilion), Kyoto; garden attributed to Soami (1471-1523). (See also Plates 42-43.)* After finding one's way through three gates and making several turnings one suddenly emerges into this bright, open space, an area of raked white sand appropriately called the Silver Terrace. It is a special experience to be long remembered. In the present photograph the dazzling

effect of the sun against white sand is still further intensified by the presence of lingering snow.

59. *Stroll garden, Shugakuin Imperial Villa, Kyoto; 17th century. (See also Plate 48.)* This is one of the three big parts into which this large garden is divided. It provides a beautiful example of one of the principal themes of Japanese landscape art, of the ability to create a new universe within a small space—the reflections of trees and sky in water. Surely the sweep of this reflection—once seen and never forgotten—is as infinite to the mind's eye as the broadest of universes.

LINKING NATURE AND ARCHITECTURE

60-63. *Verandas, Katsura Imperial Villa, Kyoto; 17th century.* Katsura might well be called the villa of verandas if it were not so many other things besides, if it were not an aggregate of so many elements all integrated to make one of the treasures of Japanese architecture. But let us return to verandas. First (Plate 60) there is the veranda formed at ground level by the overhanging main floor. Although the villa is believed to have been raised on stilts, as it were, to avoid floods, still the veranda space so created at ground level plays a definite, probably a deliberate, part in fusing the building with its garden. Then (Plate 62) on the main level there is a wide, open veranda along the whole front, supplemented by the so-called Moon Viewing Platform made of bamboo. Often wet by rain, the wooden floor of this veranda, as shown in detail in Plate 61, has weathered, doubtless by deliberate intent, to a wonderful texture of wood grain. Yet another veranda (Plate 63) has sliding doors at either side, plus a strip of straw matting to make it more a part of the house while still maintaining its affinity with the outdoors when it is thrown open.

64. *Veranda, Reiun-in, Myoshin-ji, Kyoto; 16th century.* These are the guest apartments of a priest's residence of the temple; decorated with paintings by the famed Kano Motonobu (1476-1559), this small building is often called the Motonobu Temple. A veranda looks onto a small garden, which becomes practically coextensive with the rooms, while a covered corridor leads away at the left.

65. *Seiryo-den audience hall, Kyoto Imperial Palace; 1855 reconstruction of late-8th-century original.* Within the palace complex this "Serene and Cool Chamber" was originally intended as the emperor's living quarters but came to be used for imperial audiences. Restored several times but largely retaining its original style, this gives a good idea of the palace veranda of ancient times. It was here on the veranda that lower-ranking courtiers sat during audiences, and the shapes of the pillars are hierarchical symbols, round for higher rank on the inner side and square for lower on the outer. Beyond the veranda spreads the garden.

66. *Veranda, Kinkaku-ji (Golden Pavilion), Kyoto; modern restoration of 1394 original. (See also Plate 52.)* Each of the three stories of the Golden Pavilion has a different type of veranda. The one seen here is that of the living quarters on the first floor facing onto the pond. The doors at the right deserve notice. By raising the upper halves and removing the latticework lower halves, the interior could be thrown entirely open to the pond and garden beyond.

67. *Kojo-in guest apartments, Mii-dera, Shiga Prefecture; c. 1601.* Here an L-shaped veranda permits the garden to be viewed from two angles, seeming all but to pull the pond into the building itself. Such protruding verandas also were often found in the residences of noblemen, but there they were more frequently used as entrances.

THE PILLAR AND THE MAT

68. *Pillar system, Hall of the Great Buddha, Todai-ji, Nara; 1708 reconstruction of 752 original.* Somewhat smaller in its present reconstruction than was the original, this hall housing the Great Buddha is still the largest wooden building in the world. Its 60 great pillars, measuring from 5 to 6.5 feet in diam-

eter, together with the magnificent roof glimpsed in Plate 41, give impressive shelter indeed to the colossal bronze figure, which rises to a height of 54.3 feet and weighs 452 tons. What better symbol could be found for the all-important role of the pillar in Japanese architecture?

69. *Underside of roof, Main Hall, Shinyakushi-ji, Nara; 747.* Like all early temples, this one was left unceiled. The weight of these monumental roofs was supported entirely by the pillars and the crossbeams, not by the walls, making it possible, as here, to dispense with walls entirely wherever an open space was desired.

70. *Shiro-shoin reception hall, Nishi Hongan-ji, Kyoto; believed to have originally been part of Fushimi Castle, where Hideyoshi died in 1598.* Here we look from the veranda into the great hall used for the formal entertaining of guests. A polychrome ceiling conceals the roof structure. The raised portion, where two lights shine, is for guests of higher rank—the higher his social position the deeper a person's place within the room. The bamboo barricade is to control sightseers and is not part of the architecture. Here one notes a frequent feature of Japanese spatial sequence, with a large room gradually growing darker, its innermost reaches receding into mystery. The subsequent *sukiya* style of construction was able to push the pillars back into corners and out of the way, thus giving much more flexibility to a room, but only by dispensing with such large-scale grandeur as we see here. It was also the pillar method of construction that permitted rooms such as this to be disassembled and moved to become again intact entities within a completely different building.

71. *Shishin-den enthronement hall, Kyoto Imperial Palace; 1855 reconstruction of late-8th-century original.* Used for the most important state functions, including the formal ceremony of enthronement, this hall follows the most ancient palace style in using neither *tatami* nor sliding doors. The pillars rise sturdily through floors of polished wood. The

space between the two rows of pillars is under the eaves of the building and hence is a sort of veranda. Such space was not counted in giving the area of buildings in ancient times, which is further indication of how much the Japanese consider the veranda to be part of the outdoors.

72-74. *Country merchant's house (Kusakabe residence), Gifu Prefecture; 19th century. (See also Plate 14.)* As in many large rural homes, portions of this house, like those seen here, are left unceiled. The large room in Plate 72 is the dining room. Although changing economic conditions have caused this house to be no longer used as a combined residence and place of business, the small rooms for the reception of business callers are still in evidence (Plates 73-74.) Although one of these is an interior room, it receives daylight from an overhead window in the gable as well as through the translucent partition. The earthen-floored entryway with its broad step leading up into the house proper is seen in Plate 74. Many simpler business transactions were conducted here, with the master spreading a cushion for the client on the step and also setting out a charcoal brazier. The structural framework of the house is clearly visible, as is the more recent addition of electric wiring. This latter feature is commonly seen in the older rural homes, and the choice of fixtures tells much about the difficulty the Japanese have had in recent times in reconciling their older, time-sanctioned architectural traditions with modern innovations.

75-76. *Room interiors, Katsura Imperial Villa, Kyoto; 17th century.* In these living and entertainment rooms the pillars are all but concealed by the many sliding doors. In Japanese architecture such doors are called *shoji* (made of light frames covered with a single layer of thin, unpatterned white paper which is frequently changed, and usually opening to the outside) and *fusuma* (room dividers of a more durable nature, made of several layers of opaque, patterned paper or sometimes of wood). All these doors can be quickly removed from the grooves in which they slide and be stowed away, thus turning two or more rooms into a single room and leaving this spacious area—*tatami* below, wooden ceiling above, and functional pillars again much in evidence—as open to the outside as a garden pavilion. The room of Plate 75 is in the house proper, while that of Plate 76 is in a small garden building called a *chaya*. Though the word literally means "teahouse," it is to be distinguished from the small tearoom or teahouse favored by the tea cult, called *chashitsu*. The *chaya*, spacious and open and generally containing a number of rooms (one of which is usually a *chashitsu* for the tea ceremony), is more in the nature of a summerhouse used for receiving guests, for recreation, and sometimes for living. The room seen here is not as deserted as it seems; all the various pieces of furniture and equipment for entertaining are awaiting the moment of need, each in its appointed place in cupboards, shelves, and closets.

OF TEA, BAMBOO, AND MORE PILLARS

77. *Tearoom entrance, Myoki-an temple, between Osaka and Kyoto; 16th century.* Having considered the large, formal rooms of Japanese architecture, with their functional pillars often much in evidence and their large expanses of mats, we turn now to a different architectural world, that of the tearoom, which, with its *sukiya* style, was gradually to have an effect upon the formal rooms themselves.

78. *Tearoom alcove, Myoki-an temple, between Osaka and Kyoto; 16th century.* With this upretentious, almost dilapidated room—a registered national treasure of Japan, famed as the creation and one-time residence of the great tea-master Sen-no-Rikyu and as the site of lessons in tea ceremony given to Japan's military dictator Hideyoshi—we enter the world of the teahouse. Here the tearoom itself measures but two mats in area. Although teahouse design almost always follows the *tatami* system, this room is an exception in using the pillar system.

79. *Ryuko-in tearoom, Daitoku-ji, Kyoto; 17th century.* This tea chamber is in one of the priest's residences.

The simple shelving is for holding tea utensils. The tea-master sits beside the charcoal hearth in the foreground and the guests sit in the right background facing an ornamental alcove used for displaying a hanging scroll painting and a very simple, artless flower arrangement.

80. *Teigyoku-ken tearoom, Shinju-an priests' quarters, Daitoku-ji, Kyoto; 15th century. (See also Plates 44-47.)* Note the soft, diffused light from the *shoji* windows. Tearooms are deliberately kept dark to enhance the spirit of quiet contemplation in which the tea ceremony is to be conducted.

81. *Konchi-in tearoom, Nanzen-ji, Kyoto; 17th century.* Again a tea chamber attached to a priest's residence. Although only four are here visible, the room has eight small windows, each of a different design. Such details are carefully planned by the tea-master himself when creating the teahouse, and the placing of windows, often in unconventional positions, is as deliberately planned for effect as is stage lighting. The pillar method of construction makes it possible to open windows at almost any point in the walls.

82. *Tearoom entrance, Manju-in, Kyoto; 17th century.* A *fusuma* covered with white paper leads into the adjoining tea chamber. Part of the ornamental alcove of this larger room is visible at the left. The white baseboard is actually a strip of paper pasted to the mud-plaster wall and can be changed when it becomes soiled.

83. *Bamboo grove.* Such groves as this are a common sight throughout Japan. For many centuries the use of bamboo was mainly restricted to such purely utilitarian, rural purposes as fences and as supports for thatched roofs. But the tea-masters, recognizing its great beauty and usefulness and also wanting touches of rustic simplicity in their buildings, introduced bamboo widely into their teahouses, and its popularity was soon established as an important, though subsidiary, building material. For tearooms the most prized bamboo was that which had taken on a dark patina from having been used

in the thatched roofs of farmhouses, where it soon became covered with soot. Also the graceful curves of bamboo were much in accord with Japanese ideals of asymmetrical beauty.

84-87. Shoji *and transom patterns of the* sumiya *style, Kyoto.* In the *sumiya* style great attention was paid to small details such as the patterns of the framework for translucent-paper doors and the transoms above them. The moving of the pillars into corners also made possible large uninterrupted expanses of the ingenious patterns.

88-89. *Washroom, Katsura Imperial Villa, Kyoto; 17th century.* The washroom just outside the toilet room. The crossbeamed stand is for holding a washbasin. The deep hole to the left is for pouring out the used water; it is floored with sand. Any water that is spilled on the floor while washing the hands drips down through the bamboo without forming puddles on the floor.

90. *Underside of roof, Kasa-tei summerhouse, Kodai-ji, Kyoto; 16th century, originally in grounds of Hideyoshi's Fushimi Castle.* This is another *chaya.* The rustic ceiling made of bamboo and reed resembles an umbrella and gives the structure its name, Umbrella Pavilion.

91. *Gepparo summerhouse, Katsura Imperial Villa, Kyoto; 17th century.* The interior of another of the villa's famous *chaya* pavilions. Here again bamboo and reed are used for the underside of the unceiled roof, and the verandas likewise are of bamboo.

BORROWING SPACE

92-93. *Looking out from the entrance vestibule, Katsura Imperial Villa, Kyoto; 17th century.* The approach to the vestibule is by a diagonal path (barely visible at the left of Plate 92), leaving the main vista to consist of nothing but the small entry garden with a stone lantern, one tree, and a hedge. Note how this vista seems to belong to, to be but an extension of, the matted vestibule itself. The windows through which we get another perspective on the

entry garden in Plate 93 is just to the left of the door into the vestibule. The steppingstones leading off to the right give access to the garden (see Plate 37).

94. *View from veranda, Kinkaku-ji (Golden Pavilion), Kyoto; 1394.* The view from the first floor of this three-story building gives one the impression that the pond is merely an extension of the veranda. The accenting of the borders of the pond with natural stones and trees is a typical technique of Japanese gardening.

95. *View from Daisen-in priest's apartment, Daitoku-ji, Kyoto; garden attributed to Soami (1472-1523).* This garden, in the meditative Zen tradition, has often been called the highest achievement of Japanese landscape art. Sitting on the *tatami* and looking out from the inner recesses of the room, one sees how the planes of matting, wooden-floored veranda, and quiet garden beyond do indeed form a single unit of architectural space, and a quite ordinary room suddenly becomes as infinite as the world of the imagination.

96. *View from veranda, Ryoan-ji, Kyoto; garden attributed to Soami (1472-1523).* The veranda is split into two levels, leading the eye by gracious stages to the magnificent simplicity of the garden beyond, the weathered wall, and finally the "borrowed landscape."

97. *View from the study, Jiko-in, Nara Prefecture; 17th century.* Another country villa that was later turned into a temple. The building stands on a low hill overlooking a broad expanse of the fertile Yamato Plains. The main house is of the ordinary, thatch-roof type. To reach it one climbs a narrow path leading through a natural grove of trees, expecting very little from the unpretentious surroundings. But once inside the temple, a sudden and vast panorama of beauty opens before the eyes. A superb use of the borrowed-landscape and borrowed-space principles, this is also an excellent example of the fact that it was only the unusually wide openings to the outdoors permitted by the pillar method of

construction and sliding doors that made these principles possible.

98. *View from a connecting corridor, Itsukushima (Miyajima) Shrine, Hiroshima Prefecture; reconstruction along lines of original dating back at least to 811.* Here the builder has gained space for his building by borrowing not only the inlet of the sea and the mountains beyond but also the striking red torii that is such a famed Japanese monument.

RHYTHMS OF THE VERTICAL PLANE

99-100. *Kiyomizu Temple, Kyoto; 17th-century reconstruction of early-9th-century original.* The vertical plane begins with the pillars, the basic framework. In its unadorned, unfilled-in state, as seen in the foundations for the platform of this hillside temple, the framework can in itself be a thing of beauty, with a play of shadows to produce the illusion of a plane. The arrangement of this temple complex also is interesting; distributed along a flexible axis and following the contours of the terrain, the buildings themselves seem to form a stroll garden in their own right.

101-102. *Sambutsu-ji temple, Tottori Prefecture.* An out-of-the-way mountain temple of uncertain history, this nevertheless provides an excellent example of a rudimentary use of the pillar. Built into an irregular cliff, the varying lengths of the supporting pillars have a rhythm all their own.

103. *Shoso-in treasure house, Todai-ji, Nara; late 8th century. (See also Plates 9-10.)* A combination of pillar supports and rough-textured facade, here the rhythm is one of primitive times, summoning up visions of ancient heroes and demigods.

104. *Kyoto Imperial Palace; 1855 reconstruction of late-8th-century original.* This gives a good idea of the vertical-plane rhythms of the early palace style— white plaster walls (probably originally only boards) and grid-work doors between heavy pillars. The wooden doors are hinged at the tops and swing inward to throw the room open to the outside.

The small window under the veranda is to ventilate against dampness.

105-106. *Gokuraku-bo priests' quarters, Gango-ji, Nara Prefecture; 13th century or earlier.* Early temples such as this had the priests' quarters under a single roof instead of in separate houses as later became customary. Here one dwelling unit, consisting of three rooms for living and sleeping (the communal dining room was in a separate building), occupied the space between each pair of pillars. The two views show the storm shutters (unusual in that they fold rather than slide) open and closed, providing an excellent example of the various rhythms that can be produced by changes in fittings.

107. *Small Abbot's Quarters, Myoshin-ji, Kyoto; 17th century.* A view of the side of the living quarters of the head priest. If it can be said that the effectiveness of the rhythm of Plates 105-106 depends upon balanced repetition, here it is asymmetrical imperfection that creates a distinctively beautiful harmony of its own.

108. *Katsura Imperial Villa, Kyoto; 17th century.* This is the front of the newest of the three parts of this remarkable villa. Unlike the older part seen in Plate 62, here the pillars are very widely spaced, with four *shoji* between each pair. The wooden storm shutters, one of which can be seen at the far left, are stored out of sight in shutter boxes like the one seen at the far right. In modern houses there are also sliding glass doors between the *shoji* and the shutters.

109. *Village house (Yoshimura residence), near Osaka; 17th century.* This was the home of a village head in late feudal times. As is the case with almost all private homes, the vertical plane gains its rhythm from asymmetry, from the many compromises needed to make the house functional. For example, the smaller window at the right serves both to give light inside and to allow someone inside the house to see who is calling at the front door (just outside the photograph at the right), while the tiny window above it serves for ventilation. The large *shoji*

at the left open onto the main sitting room where guests are received. There is a veranda just in front of this room, and the bars at its outer edge give some privacy to the room within while the veranda also serves as an auxiliary access to the room (note the stone step at the far left where footgear is left before stepping up). All these varied functions in ensemble have produced the distinctive vertical-plane rhythms of this facade.

110. *Farmhouse (Sato residence), Niigata Prefecture; 19th century.* A middle-class farmhouse with a thatched roof, its peak protected by bark shingles. One enters the usual earthen-floored room through the doorway at the right; this room runs the length of the house to the back yard and is flanked by the *tatami* living rooms on the left and storerooms on the right. The facade is, again, an ensemble of happy, functional compromises, beginning with the black wainscoting to protect the white walls from being splashed with the mud of the street.

THE ROOF AS SYMBOL

111-112. *Shrine gable, Grand Shrine of Izumo, Shimane Prefecture; 18th-century reduced-scale reconstruction in traditional primitive style.* The roof is shingled with the traditional cypress bark, but the addition of a monumental tile at the gable peak, not found in purer examples of the native Japanese style such as the Grand Shrine of Ise, points to inroads of Chinese influence at some stage in the many reconstructions. Note the deep overhang of the eaves to protect the building from rain.

113. *Shrine gable, Inner Precincts, Grand Shrine of Ise, Mie Prefecture; reconstruction of 3rd(?)-century original.* One of the rice storehouses in the shrine compound. Again the roof is of cypress-bark shingles, with a deep overhang. The bargeboards extend in a V above the roof ridge to form the so-called *chigi*, a characteristic of primitive Japanese roofs which was continued even after, as in Plate 112, it had lost structural meaning and was merely added decoration. The status-symbol quality of roofs is

clearly seen in the story of a 5th-century emperor who became so incensed at seeing these roof decorations, which were then used on imperial dwellings also, on the roof of a local chieftain that he threatened to raze the house.

114. *Farmhouse gable, Lake Biwa, Shiga Prefecture; 18th century.* Most Japanese farmhouses have roofs of thatch, although in recent times tile and even corrugated iron have gained in favor. The triangular opening in the gable peak is for letting out smoke from the stoves and hearths used in the house, as in many primitive buildings in other cultures. Farmhouse roofs vary greatly in shape and style according to their regional locations, and in scale according to the owner's economic condition.

115-116. *Temple roofs, Toshodai-ji, Nara; 8th century.* The first plate shows a side view of the Main Hall. In the second plate the Main Hall is seen at the top and the Lecture Hall at the bottom. Whereas Shinto shrines are generally roofed with cypress-bark shingles and farmhouses with thatch, since ancient times the roofs of Buddhist temples, like their Chinese prototypes, have always been tiled.

117. *Castle roof lines, Matsumoto, Nagano Prefecture; 17th century.* The impressive sweep, layer upon layer, of the tiled roofs of the castle keep were doubtless planned as symbols of power and standing, to impress one's friends and frighten one's enemies.

118. *Pagoda, Muro-ji, Nara Prefecture; 824 or possibly earlier.* This small, five-story pagoda with tiled roofs stands on the highest point in the temple compound, carrying the eye always upward to heaven. It seems like a bird that has perched here at the top of the stone stairway for a moment before continuing its flight.

119. *Pagoda eaves, Daigo-ji, Kyoto; 951.* A close view of one of the early typical five-story pagodas. Note the interplay of light and shadows.

120. *Farmhouse roof, Tamugimata Village, Yamagata Prefecture; 19th century.* The curves of the ridges,

produced by the slack-string method, are particularly impressive.

121. *Farmhouse roof, Izumo district, Shimane Prefecture; 19th century*. The upward curve of the gables is typical of the district. Certainly roofs such as this and the preceding one served as status symbols for their owners.

122. *Farmhouse roofs, Hida-Katsura Village, Gifu Prefecture; 18th-19th centuries*. This thatch-roofed farmhouse, deep in the mountains, is one of the gigantic kind typical of the region in which many blood-related families live together under one huge roof, with an attic used for raising silkworms. Here the dew on the roof is evaporating into vapor in the morning sun.

123. *Urban roofs, village in the Yamato Plains, Nara Prefecture*. A typical village pattern of the Yamato Plains. Each residence consists of a courtyard surrounded by the main house, the gatehouse, and various warehouses and storehouses. Sometimes there is a small garden in one corner of the courtyard, usually in front of the reception room, while the rest of the courtyard is used for drying crops. The pattern of urban roofs one after the other, all in soft grays, is a typical part of the Japanese scene.

MISCELLANEOUS

124. *Katsura Imperial Villa, Kyoto; 17th century*. A final, aerial view of this remarkable creation of architectural space about which we have had much to say in the pages of this book.

125. *Nijo Detached Palace, Kyoto; 17th century and later*. This former Kyoto castle-residence of the military rulers of the country, who ruled from Tokyo (then called Edo), is a complex of architectural note. It consists of two main enclosures surrounded by moats. The residential area in the upper part of the photograph was built in the 17th century, its zigzag arrangement of buildings being reminiscent of the Katsura Imperial Villa. The castle keep stood in the lower enclosure but was destroyed by fire. The buildings that stand there now, formerly a nobleman's residence, were brought to the site and reassembled in 1893.

126. *Village in the Yamato Plains, Nara Prefecture*. Aptly described as "the grand theater of early Japanese history," the Yamato Plains around Kyoto and Nara were the cradle of Japanese culture, no less of architecture than of all the early arts and crafts.

127. *City of Nara, founded 710*. Nara was Japan's capital from 710 to 784, the first city built along Chinese models with the streets regularly laid out, and from this nucleus the new developments in architecture made their way gradually throughout the land. The people who today live closely packed in these wooden houses are descendants of the creators of the architectural tradition we have been considering. Even though they may live in the uneasy fear of seeing their homes destroyed by fire or earthquake, still it is here, in this and the many other cities of Japan, that the future of Japanese architecture is now being fashioned.

128. *Pillar of Japanese cypress*. Our last plate harks back to our first to show the two favorite woods of Japanese architecture. In the first we saw the lordly tree as it exists in nature, while here it is serving its all-important function as a pillar—a man-made structural element that yet seems to have something about it of nature's inevitable rightness. But this does not bring us back again to the beginning in our architectural quest: architecture is never a closed circle. Always it is on the move, sometimes progressing, sometimes retrogressing. It is up to each generation to determine in which direction it will move.

INDEX TO PLATES

(References are to plate numbers)